"Occasionally, a book comes along that a field d
Professional Learning is such a book. It is clear, acc
Cutting through the vast literature on professiona
ultimate end game is making a difference to learner
read."

—**Professor Alma Harris**, University of Bath, UK

"Deborah Netolicky's *Transformational Professional Learning* is a must-read for anyone with an interest in developing authentic and impactful professional learning for themselves and for teachers and school leaders. As a pracademic, Netolicky expertly weaves together thoughtful and thorough analyses of existing international research literatures, her own original research findings, and her in-depth expertise from an extensive career as a teacher and school leader. Few books accomplish the complex and sophisticated task of genuinely bringing together new research insights and new practical applications; this book achieves this and more to create new possibilities for understanding and action. *Transformation Professional Learning* avoids one size fits all solutions, magic bullets, and artificial polarisations that characterise much educational debate to produce a book that places the complexity, identity, work, voices, and humanity of educators at the centre of professional learning to benefit their own development and the learning of the students they serve."

— **Carol Campbell**, Associate Professor, Ontario Institute for Studies in Education, University of Toronto, Canada

"If we want to produce ambitious changes in student learning goals, we will need to reimagine and invigorate new forms for learning for the adults who are striving to produce these outcomes. In this compact and timely book, Deborah Netolicky deftly balances research summaries of effective professional learning with vivid stories from the field that illustrate these ideas at work."

—**Bruce Wellman**, Co-Director, MiraVia LLC, USA

"In this comprehensive guidebook for getting the most from the many different kinds of professional development initiatives, Dr Deborah Netolicky begins by showing how to identify and engage better with customary professional learning that is mostly *informational* in nature. Netolicky then leads readers into *transformational* professional learning—that is, learning that both challenges and also supports professionals in examining and sometimes changing their beliefs, attitudes and values that govern behaviours and drive improvement to professional practice. Netolicky's own rich and deep experiences, as a researching educational leader and as professional developer, make this wonderful compendium extraordinarily helpful, practical, and meaningful. *Transformational Professional Learning* is a treasure chest of ideas, practices, and strategies that are vitally important to helping schools to become better places of learning, growth, and development for adults as well as for children."

—**Professor Ellie Drago-Severson**, Teachers College, Columbia University, USA

"Deborah Netolicky's comprehensive, research-informed book on teacher professional learning effectively bridges the research-practice divide to provide an essential resource for teachers and school leaders. Written in an accessible, conversational style, the book locates current thinking about teacher professional learning in Australian schools within broader national and international contexts, and highlights the complexity of this field in which there are no 'silver bullets'. Scholarly and practical, Netolicky's book argues for an expansive and generative understanding of teacher professional learning, shaped and tailored differently for teachers with many and varied learning needs working in radically different contexts."

—**Nicole Mockler**, Associate Professor, University of Sydney, Australia

"This is a valuable book because it is written from a new perspective. Deborah Netolicky's position as a 'pracademic' allows her to address many of the tensions and recognise the opportunities inherent in teachers' professional learning. The book extends an invitation to engage with dimensions of practice alongside the author's analysis of her own and others' research. The insights offered are essential for those working in complex spaces where children and young peoples' learning is at the forefront, but in which professional learning is critical."

—**Professor Rachel Lofthouse**, Carnegie School of Education,
Leeds Beckett University, UK

"Improving what people do in schools is a key to better student learning. In this book, Deborah Netolicky shares her experiences as teacher, leader and researcher and shows, using concrete examples, how to make the most out of professional learning for the benefit of all children."

—**Pasi Sahlberg**, Gonski Institute for Education, UNSW, Australia

Transformational Professional Learning

Emerging from an education world that sees professional learning as a tool to positively shape teaching practice in order to improve student learning, *Transformational Professional Learning* elucidates professional learning that is transformational for teachers, school leaders, and schools.

Written from the unique 'pracademic' perspective of an author who is herself a practising teacher, school leader, and researcher, this book articulates the why and the what of professional learning. It acts as a bridge between research and practice by weaving scholarly literature together with the lived experience of the author and with the voices of those working in schools. It covers topics from conferences, coaching, and collaboration, to teacher standards and leadership of professional learning.

This book questions the ways in which professional learning is often wielded in educational settings and shows where teachers, school leaders, system leaders, and researchers can best invest their time and resources in order to support and develop the individuals, teams, and cultures in schools. It will be of great interest to teachers, leaders within schools, staff responsible for professional learning in school contexts, professional learning consultants, professional learning providers, and education researchers.

Deborah M. Netolicky has 20 years of experience in teaching and school leadership in Australia and the UK. She has received national and international awards for her leadership, research, and writing. Deborah blogs at theedufla neuse.com, tweets as @debsnet, and co-edited *Flip the System Australia: What Matters in Education* (Routledge 2018).

Transformational Professional Learning

Making a Difference in Schools

Deborah M. Netolicky

Routledge
Taylor & Francis Group

LONDON AND NEW YORK

First published 2020
by Routledge
2 Park Square, Milton Park, Abingdon, Oxon OX14 4RN

and by Routledge
52 Vanderbilt Avenue, New York, NY 10017

Routledge is an imprint of the Taylor & Francis Group, an informa business

© 2020 Deborah M. Netolicky

British Library Cataloguing-in-Publication Data
A catalogue record for this book is available from the British
Library

Library of Congress Cataloging-in-Publication Data
A catalog record has been requested for this book

ISBN: 978-0-367-34172-5 (hbk)
ISBN: 978-0-367-34174-9 (pbk)
ISBN: 978-0-429-32427-7 (ebk)

Typeset in Bembo
by Swales & Willis, Exeter, Devon, UK

Printed and bound by CPI Group (UK) Ltd, Croydon, CR0 4YY

To my three favourites
Nic, Harry, and Jesse.

Contents

Tables

Foreword

Most Forewords begin with an invited expert in the twilight of their professional lives, setting out his or her wisdom on the state of the field that the ensuing text of the book addresses. Eventually, in the last two or three paragraphs, the expert then gets around to saying a few kind things about the book itself.

But in this case, we need to turn things around. This is, simply, an extraordinary book. I have never seen anything quite like it. I have read books by outstanding researchers, some of them former teachers, myself (at my best) included, who have and who can convey empathy and a studied grasp of the work of teachers and how it connects to their lives and their worlds. I have also read very engaging books by teachers and leaders about their own worlds and work that are full of ideas, absorbing anecdotes, practical wisdom, and a sprinkling of insights from researchers and thought leaders in the academic world to back them up.

This book is something else, though. As a synthesis of the field of professional learning and a critical exploration of its less fashionable and more unusual aspects—like self-directed learning, or attending courses—I can recall scarcely any better ones in the academic community itself. Unlike many researchers who collate all the evidence before them and draw circumspect conclusions about what it all means, Deborah Netolicky goes further and, in her own voice, as both academic and practitioner, she expresses it all from a constructively critical and also professionally candid perspective.

At the same time, in each of the chapters, she lays out her own experience as a researcher, teacher, and leader. Come away from this and you'll not only be able to take with you a few bullet points, tips, and plans, but you'll know exactly what a professional learning plan can actually look like in practice, what sorts of choices you can best offer your staff in a balanced menu of offerings that connects the power of personal learning to that of the school, and how you can set about building a coaching relationship that is suitably challenging without being oppressive.

Netolicky is positive and balanced. Keynote speakers outside the school can and indeed do have value alongside shared staff development within the school. University courses and graduate degrees are not always a waste of time. The best professional learning isn't often or always fun – and from time to time may be downright uncomfortable. Twitter is not just an indulgence or a distraction.

And some of the best professional learning you'll ever get as a teacher might not be deliberate or planned at all – facing a crisis, having a child, enduring a bad leader, and so on. And Netolicky also has a healthy skepticism about copying things from other systems, about "opportunists with questionable agendas," and about administrators who micro-manage their staff's development choices on the one hand, or show no interest in them at all on the other. This makes this terrific book both practical and provocative at one and the same time.

Deborah Netolicky is part of a new breed of thought leader in education known as the *pracademic*. My autocorrect function on my laptop sometimes translates this as paramedic!! In fact, the two words and the worlds they capture are not all that far apart.

Pracademics span the worlds of research and practice. On the one hand, they may be researchers with a good feel for practice, a willingness to engage with practitioners on equal and reciprocal terms, and a readiness to take a strategic as well as intellectual approach to improvement. There have always been a number of scholars around with this orientation – and I'd be glad to count myself among them. It's really a question of preference and orientation as well as being prepared to endure sometimes the disapproving stance of researchers who see themselves as more 'pure' and detached in the stance that they take.

Coming in from the other side is much harder. Of course, for years, teachers have written curriculum textbooks. Past, and less frequently, current principals like Eric Sheninger and the late Rick Dufour in the US, or Tom Sherrington and Andy Buck in the UK (all men, I realise), will write and talk about their own experiences with professional learning communities, introducing technology, or managing change and innovation, for example, and they'll draw on the ideas and research of academic thought leaders as they do so.

But it's much harder for teachers to take this bold step. Criticisms of government policy might constitute a breach of contract and lead them to lose their jobs. Principals might try to quell teachers' voices if their writing and speaking jeopardises the reputation of their schools, or simply outshines them, as principals. And schools, as much as universities, are sadly, riddled with envy, and with the belief, in a relatively flat career structure, that no teacher should hog the stage more than any other, or even at all.

The game is changing though – for three reasons. First, is the paradoxical effect of markets. Although markets create inequities between students and schools, they also do exactly what they are supposed to do and create space for greater freedom too, at least for some. In the right kind of school, with the right leader, there is no big, defensive bureaucracy to keep innovative teachers in their place, or hold them back. So some teachers, under benign or inspirational principals, can step forward, be innovative and bold, and even criticise government policies, and the weakening of old bureaucracies protects them from external sanction or top-down censorship. (Of course, the strangulating effects of big bureaucracies can, under controlling principals, also be replaced by petty, small school tyrannies, so the opportunities for finding and expressing your public and professional voice as a teacher are not distributed fairly or equally).

Second, the movement over the past decades to construct a more differentiated teacher career and the growth of formal and informal teacher leadership is encouraging and enabling more teachers to step out and step forward including into a wider world of professional learning and development as well as innovation. Teachers are getting chances to become teacher-preneurs, to develop and express their own voice and even develop a market and an income for their ideas, just as some academics do.

Third is the impact of social media, globalisation, blogging and short reads; not just scholarly articles and long reads. This kind of world can intersect more easily with a continuing teacher career, especially one that doesn't involve being full-on with a full-load of classes and subjects all the time. Presence on the web means ability to access ideas quickly rather than trudging over to a distant library, to circulate ideas fast on Twitter chat, Skype, or Zoom, and to become producers as well as consumers of knowledge. This might irritate a few purist academics who could rightly feel aggrieved that three to five years of rigorous research are accorded no greater value than a rapidly assembled blog or two. But then again, teachers could also complain that years of developing good practice are too easily hijacked or colonised by researchers like myself who get citations and accolades by writing about the hard work that other people do rather than giving educators a chance and a platform to write about it themselves.

Whichever is the case, the pracademic is here to stay, and Deborah Netolicky is providing us with an excellent example of what we can uniquely learn from this new kind of voice that has come onto the modern educational landscape.

Andy Hargreaves
April 2019

Acknowledgements

This book would not be possible without the contributions of generous and often uncelebrated teachers and school leaders, including those who participated in my PhD study, and those with whom I have worked and from whom I have learned during my 20 year teaching career. These include the leaders who have supported me in my teaching and leadership, and colleagues who have inspired, buoyed, and encouraged me. These are those individuals working in our schools who teach and care for the students in their classrooms, and for one another, every day. This is cognitively challenging and emotionally taxing work. Many teachers and school leaders put their students' needs ahead of their own, with far reaching impacts on their own lives and wellbeing. The indelible imprint of other educators on my own life and work comes through in the chapters of this book.

I acknowledge the collaborators, writerly friends, and colleagues who have helped me to realise that I have something to say, and the capacity and the courage to say it. This network includes my PhD supervisors Judy McCallum and Amanda Woods-McConney. It includes generous professors who give of their expertise in the public realm. It includes authors with whom I have co-written. It includes the many teachers, school leaders, and academics who have connected with me on Twitter and via my blog, challenging my thinking and engaging me in robust conversations around teaching, learning, education, and research. Through these partnerships and collaborations, I have tested out ideas, been encouraged to think and write differently, and built relationships with those who think and write differently to me. These connections have made me a better writer, a better thinker, a better teacher, and a better leader.

Thank you especially to those who generously read all or part of this book during the writing process, and provided me with helpful and honest feedback: Carol Campbell, Andy Hargreaves, Christine Grice, Gary Jones, Rachel Lofthouse, Nicole Mockler, Chris Munro, Pasi Sahlberg, Bruce Wellman, my husband Nic Hayes, and my Routledge commissioning editor Vilija Stephens. This book is better for it.

Ultimately the work and professional learning we do in education is about the students and communities we serve. I acknowledge the many students I have taught over the last 20 years, and their part in my own being and becoming as a learner, a teacher, and a leader.

Introduction
About this book

Why this book

Professional learning is big business. As a school leader who leads professional learning and staff development at my school, my inbox is always bursting with emails about professional learning courses, conferences, books, consultants, and companies. In itself, this kind of electronic onslaught reminds teachers and schools that we should be doing more, better. We should be going further and jumping higher. We should be staying ahead of the curve and operating at the bleeding edge of education trends. The horizon is perpetually out of reach. Everyone has a perspective to sell. Companies compete to advertise and sell their wares. *We have the answer!* they cry; the answer to helping teachers get better, do better, know more, perform more competently, top those tests, know their students. Those from outside schools often sell answers to perceived education problems. Experts are flown in from different countries to advise teachers and school leaders how to do things better. *Fly in Expert A! They have shiny, easy Solution B!* Piecemeal initiatives are inserted into sometimes inappropriate school contexts because they are seen as 'best practice' somewhere. *Be like Country X who performs well on Test Y. They must be doing it right!*

But schools, even in the same country, are different. States, districts, and suburbs are different. Social and economic conditions are different. Funding and resourcing are different. There is no one-size-fits-all magic solution, and perhaps not even a clear problem that needs solving, despite the relentless deficit view of the teaching profession as a dehumanised thing that needs to be fixed. As just about everyone in education says: context matters.

Teachers and leaders currently working in schools around the world can attest to the intense pressures to perform in ways that appear good to the outside world, while potentially harming the experiences and wellbeing of teachers and students. I was chatting to one of my son's teachers about the visible work that teachers do for show, rather than to positively influence student learning. She called this "*looking good* instead of *doing good.*" She pointed out that teachers and schools are expected to do things that appear impressive to parents, observers, school assessors, standardised test measures, or the community, rather than focusing on what is really going to make a difference to student learning.

Professional learning has to some extent become another stick wielded to discipline teachers, and a prescription applied to fix teachers. This results in artificial veneers of learning and improvement, performance against questionable measures, and professional learning that is ineffective in transforming beliefs and practices. Cultures of fear, competition, alienation, and compliance are the result of approaching teacher development with a deficit view and an agenda that encourages artificial high-stakes performance against visible, measurable accountabilities. Professional development initiatives benefit from being based in trust, collaboration, and building the professional learning culture of schools, even if these things are hard to measure. Professional learning should be about doing good, not looking good. It should be about ongoing growth, not ticking boxes, accruing hours, or performing learning in manufactured ways.

This book makes the case for professional learning that positively shapes teacher practices that improve student learning. It frames transformational learning as the heart of professional development efforts in schools. Such learning—that develops the adults and children in our schools, and that influences the cultures of schools and the teaching profession as a whole—taps into who educators see and feel they are in their classrooms and the ways that those perceptions affect their beliefs, thoughts, and behaviours.

Why this author

The education world is bursting at the seams with books about professional learning. They are ubiquitous and almost countless. They have been written by a range of different stakeholders such as academics, consultants, and educators who have previously worked in schools. The voices of practitioners can sometimes be heard in the stories education consultants tell, or the data scholars generate alongside those working in schools. Practitioner voices emerge through the cracks of scholarship or between the lines of think tank or media reports. Rarely are practising teachers those commentating publicly on education, or writing books about education (textbooks aside). Rarely is a book about professional learning written by a practising teacher and school leader.

This *is* a book about professional learning by a teacher and school leader, written for teachers and school leaders. I have taught in high schools—in Perth, Melbourne, and London—for 20 years. I have been a school leader for almost as long, since my second year of teaching when I was appointed as head of middle school English. Since then I have led faculties, whole school strategic projects, pedagogy, the school library, research, and professional learning, across various roles in various schools. In my current daily work as a full-time teacher and school leader, I teach students in English and Literature classrooms and lead professional learning, research, and pedagogy, in my Pre-Kindergarten to Year 12 school in Perth, Western Australia. My voice comes from within the education system. Writing as a practitioner means that I am firmly embedded in what it feels like to be a cog in the school reform wheel, a participant in professional learning, and a leader of professional learning. No doubt my cynicism around corporate 'silver bullet' solutions to education 'problems,' often constructed by those not working in schools, comes through in my writing.

Even more rarely is a book about professional learning written from the *pracademic* perspective of someone who sits bestride both the practitioner world of education, and the scholarly world of research. Since completing my PhD in 2016, alongside my school day job I continue the research and academic writing that began with my PhD, with a particular focus on the professional learning of teachers and how this interacts and intersects with the emotional and human aspects of teaching and leading in schools. In the research part of my life I am an honorary research associate, an unpaid adjunct. This means there is no financial reward or professional expectation that I engage in the world of academic publishing, but it also liberatingly means that I am not bound by the expectations of the university in terms of academic output. I am free to write and research on my own terms, in ways that best inform the work I do on a daily basis in my school. My dual roles inform one another. My hybridity gives me a perspective quite different from those who commentate or advise from the sidelines. I am at once enthusiastic about professional learning for educators, and protective of the teaching profession who so often are told that we must comply with particular professional learning expectations and are evaluated according to ambiguous standards. What I do every day in my lessons, meetings, professional conversations, and operational work, influences how I interpret education research. And the research I read and undertake influences my understanding of my daily work at school.

So, the unique perspective I bring to the field of professional learning is one of boundary-spanning teacher-leader-researcher who works to bridge the gap between research and practice. In the structure and writing of this book I model the way that I bring the lens of practising teacher and school leader to research, and bring a research lens to my daily work. I connect the dots between scholarly and practical domains, to operate in the space (or as the bridge) between the world of education research and that of classroom and school. This bridging work brings a research lens to schools, where teachers and school leaders enact theory into practice, tempered by their wisdom of practice and the emotional and human elements of education that shape their behaviours each day.

This book draws back the curtain on professional learning research and practice in order to synthesise a wide range of perspectives and make these accessible to the teaching profession. On the one hand it summarises much of what is currently known about professional learning, sharing scholarly voices usually located behind a pay wall or an expensive book price tag. It additionally draws upon empirical research and lived experience to breathe life and humanity into the world of professional learning for classroom teachers and school leaders, including often-forgotten middle leaders. I share my own perspective, too, informed by tacit lived experience as an educator and qualitative researcher. In this way the book is simultaneously evidence-based, research-informed, and values the experiences and voices of practitioners.

I have not written this book via a series of tips, frequently asked questions, bullet pointed lists, or diagrams. I haven't dumbed down or oversimplified research in order to make it accessible to teachers and school leaders. I respect the profession of which I am a part, and the individuals working tirelessly in schools each and every day. I know we are busy and time poor, but we are also thoughtful, intelligent, skilled practitioners who think deeply about our work, are experts at our craft, and are capable of interpreting text that grapples with complexities, nuances, and contestations. This book is an antidote to the endless streams of emails about professional development and piles of envelopes stuffed full of conference flyers for professional learning opportunities. It makes sense of current theory and practice of professional learning for those researching and working in schools, including those in classrooms and those leading schools. The literature discussed in this book situates it within a robust worldwide conversation around the way that professional learning should be considered and enacted for teachers and in schools. It reveals that many of the ways we grow and change as professionals can be found by ourselves, with our colleagues, in our schools, and in our daily work. This kind of teacher-reclaimed professional learning doesn't require windowless conference rooms or fancy catering, but it does need time, resourcing, intentionality, and structure.

This book weaves together international perspectives with my unique Australian context, bringing an Australian lens to the field of professional learning. As my co-editors and I wrote in *Flip the System Australia: What matters in education* (Netolicky et al., 2019), Australia is a diverse nation whose education system is influenced by its Indigenous heritage, its colonial past, its vast geography, and global movements towards education cultures of blame and hyper accountability. Australia is often perceived as isolated 'down under,' and somewhere that would benefit from copying apparently high performing school systems from elsewhere (anywhere from Finland to Canada, Shanghai, or Kazakhstan, depending on the current media headline or edu-tourism favourite). But theory and practice in Australian education have much to offer the rest of the world. This book is, in a small way, a speaking out of Australian theory and practice into the international education sphere.

This book contributes to identified areas for further research in the arena of professional learning: the relationships of teacher professional learning with quality teaching, teacher collaboration, teacher leadership, and school leadership (Zammit et al., 2007); and the effect of school reforms on teachers themselves (Yoon et al., 2007) and on leaders. It interrogates and takes seriously, as argued for by Fred Korthagen (2017), the tacit, multi-dimensional nature of teacher learning, connecting the personal with the professional and the emotional with the cognitive. It proposes professional learning that is based on trusting the capacities of teachers, and adequately resourcing growth-focused professional learning opportunities. This book provides those working in and researching schools with a detailed overview of the professional learning landscape, so that they can apply research, theory, and insights from current scholarship and practice, to their decision making.

Who might read this book

This book draws together threads from practice and research in ways that are useful for those studying professional learning, but especially to those who are leading professional learning in schools or who are themselves teachers reflecting on growing their own practice. I have written this book with teachers and school leaders in mind. My aim in exploring professional learning for educators is not one based in accountabilities or deficit models of practice that diminish teacher agency. Rather, this book is a call to empower educators, to treat them as intelligent professionals, and to encourage them to reclaim the field of professional learning, for the teaching profession.

The book may also be of interest to scholars and policymakers as it explores not only *why* we need to invest in, research, and talk about professional learning for educators, but also *how* and *on what* we might best spend money, time, and resources. It provides a foundation for making decisions around professional learning from the policymaking room to the classroom.

Defining professional learning

For the purpose of this book, *professional learning* has been used to describe any experience of educator learning, including what some call *professional development, PD* (professional development), or *CPD* (continuing professional development). That is, professional learning encompasses those activities packaged as professional learning experiences for educators, such as talks, courses, and conferences. It also includes other times when educators learn, and that influence their lives and work. This reflects Helen Timperley et al.'s (2007) definition of professional development as the delivery of activities and processes, and professional learning as the internal process of creating knowledge and expertise.

This book situates professional learning as part of the process of professional *becoming*, which creates shifts in knowledge, practice, or identity (Mockler, 2013). This book is concerned with *transformational learning*—discussed in more detail in Chapter 1—for education professionals. Transformational learning shifts beliefs, and thereby behaviours of professionals. It is tied to an individual's personal and professional identity. It actively shifts cognition, emotion, and capacity (Drago-Severson, 2009). It is concerned with not just *what* someone knows and can do, but with their *ways of* knowing (Drago-Severson & Blum-DeStefano, 2018). What is shaped in transformational professional learning is how educators know and their internal capacities for knowing, doing, and being.

Why professional learning

Professional learning is identified as a crucial field in the international education context and as a tool of performance improvement due to some core assumptions. These assumptions include the following.

- At the centre of schooling is the student and student achievement. It is student learning, students' experience of schooling, and students' current and future selves, that are the core business of education.
- The adults working in those schools and systems, and their learning, directly impact on the students in their care. Teachers' teaching is correlated to students' learning.
- The learning and development of teachers is a site for improving teachers' teaching in order to improve schools, improve teaching, and thereby improve student achievement. If teachers develop expertise in the craft of teaching, and knowledge about what teaching strategies have the most positive impact on student learning, student achievement will improve.

The argument goes that differences in teachers make a difference to student learning (Australian Institute for Teaching and School Leadership (AITSL), 2018; Cordingley, 2015; Wiliam, 2016, 2018), effective professional learning is seen as crucial to developing quality teachers (Baguley & Kerby, 2012; Desimone et al., 2002). And investing in teacher professional development has great potential for improving student achievement (Drago-Severson, 2012; Wiliam, 2018; Yoon et al., 2007). Linda Darling-Hammond et al. (2009) note that,

> professional learning can have a powerful effect on teacher skills and knowledge and on student learning if it is sustained over time, focused on important content, and embedded in the work of professional learning communities that support ongoing improvements in teachers' practice (p. 7).

Laura Desimone (2009) suggests a link between effective professional learning and the following factors: increased teacher knowledge and skills; changes in teacher attitudes and beliefs; consequent change in instruction; and resulting improved student learning.

Students have been found to make more progress in some classrooms than in others due to the individual teacher (Wiliam, 2018). One Queensland study (Leigh, 2010), for instance, found considerable differences in student performance depending on the teacher. Based on a dataset of 10,000 Australian school teachers and over 90,000 students, Andrew Leigh argues that a student with an 'excellent' teacher could achieve in a half year what a student with a 'poor quality' teacher could achieve in a full year. A study in the Netherlands (van Kuijk et al., 2016) found students whose teachers had received a professional learning intervention aimed at improving student reading comprehension performed at a level more than half a year ahead of students whose teachers had not received the professional learning. Here professional learning is seen as capable of improving teacher's teaching in order to positively impact on student learning and achievement.

While there are necessary cautions when considering the influence of professional learning on teaching and student learning (explored in Chapter 1), professional learning is widely seen to benefit students and teachers. Scholars and practitioners consequently call for particular types of professional learning and collaboration as levers to improve teaching and teachers, and thereby schools and the education system. A focus on the teacher as central protagonist in student achievement has a significant effect on the field of professional learning. The teacher quality agenda places the teacher at the nucleus of education in ways that serve corporate and political agendas, but are often unhelpful to the teaching profession and ignore a number of complex factors that affect student learning.

Teacher quality, accountability, and education short termism

Teacher quality, a focus on accountability, and short term thinking are drivers of professional learning for teachers and school leaders. They are, however, as Michael Fullan (2011) would argue, the wrong drivers. The teacher quality agenda is based upon the premise that if teachers improve, student learning and achievement improves. In 1996, Christine O'Hanlon (1996) called *quality* a significant new word in the political rhetoric of education. She noted its evolution from industrial and commercial contexts, and its positioning of people as objects, which is perhaps why teachers find the term 'teacher quality' so dehumanising. Through this lens, teaching is treated as a list of competencies to be audited, correlated with pupil outcomes, and measured on standardised tests (Connell, 2009). Much professional learning reform focuses on the 'quality' of teachers, founded on statements such as that from the Organisation for Economic Cooperation and Development (OECD) that "the quality of an education system cannot exceed the quality of its teachers and principals, since student learning is ultimately the product of what goes on in classrooms" (2010, p. 4). What has followed is a focus on teacher education, recruitment, certification, regulation, and professional learning that aims or claims to 'improve' the apparent 'quality' of teaching and teachers, as though the profession were a thing to be repaired or a home to be renovated.

The teacher quality agenda is impelled by economic drivers in which countries are expected to develop their knowledge economy (Call, 2018). Despite the best of intentions to use professional learning to serve vital student outcomes, policymakers motivated by global and economic forces remain fixated on narrow measures for holding schools accountable for student learning (Lingard et al., 2016). As part of this agenda, education is wrapped up in visible politics, visible performance, and visible measurement. Politicians are expected to enact swift political action, and this can override comprehensive approaches to reform and a nuanced understanding of what constitutes evidence (Lewis & Hogan, 2016). Bob Burstow (2018) points out that, in England, Education Secretaries spend an average of two years in office. The short political cycle means that politicians chase votes and election wins instead of a longer game in the education space. Short term thinking, combined with *fast policy* that takes a 'shoot first and ask questions later' approach (Lewis & Hogan, 2016), means that education decisions, including those involving professional learning, are made in a hurry, or pre-answered before conditions and rigorous evidence are taken into account. Education solutions, including via professional learning, are presumed to be universal and are oversimplified (Lewis & Hogan, 2016).

Because in educational contexts the professional development of educators is seen as central to improving school effectiveness and driving up measurable outcomes, there is a danger that professional learning becomes dominated by improvement agendas (Stevenson, 2019). The risk is that improvement agendas can focus on measurement as an end in itself, wielded as a tool for governance, dehumanised judgement (of students, teachers, leaders, schools, and systems), comparison, and often public accountabilities. Countries are judged against international tests, but envying the performance of other countries is toxic (Sellar et al., 2017). Media headlines in the USA, the UK, and Europe use Programme for International Student Assessment (PISA) results to claim that education systems are 'acing' and 'topping' tests, or 'failing' and 'losing' (Crehan, 2016). Schools are seen as businesses and are expected to perform against external metrics, such as Australia's National Assessment Program—Literacy and Numeracy (NAPLAN), tools that are political and also questionable in terms of measuring the effectiveness of education or providing valid comparisons. Tests like NAPLAN have unintended consequences, including excessive focus on test preparation, a narrowed curriculum, student anxiety, and gaming the test (Thompson et al., 2018). A focus on testing and comparison can dilute the moral purpose of education. It can lead to gaming the system to help data look good, rather than using data to make better decisions that benefit students, teachers, and schools.

And so, teachers and school leaders find themselves caught forever in a tumult of political agendas, media sensationalism, polarising debates, and meaningless comparisons. In very real ways the realities and experiences of schooling are shaped by education policies that use language to create a reality that privileges certain ideas while excluding others (Ball, 2017). Meanwhile, educators are measured and punished, rather than trusted, nurtured, or given a voice in reform. The teaching profession is increasingly distanced from national policymaking processes (Savage & Lingard, 2018). Teachers, and even students, become objects of policy, and pawns used in games of politics, rather than agents of teaching and learning. Teachers are disciplined within audit and performance mechanisms, resulting in teachers having less and less autonomy and professional discretion in their work (Keddie, 2017; Waite, 2016). Policies that focus on accountability—like linking teacher or leader pay to student test performance—alienate practitioners, undermine the profession, and create fear and isolation.

Yet examples of 'teacher quality' rhetoric abound. Countries around the globe drive the teacher quality agenda through policy and practice. England's *The importance of teaching* white paper (Department of Education England, 2010) positions the quality of teachers and teaching as "the most important factor in determining how well children do" (p. 9), rather than considering those factors that influence student learning and achievement that are out of a school's or a teacher's control, such as the socioeconomic status of a community, or the amount of reading that happened in the home during a child's early years, or a student's parents' education, or the home or community environment. Initiatives like the USA's *No Child Left Behind Act* (Congress, 2001), the introduction of professional standards for teachers in England (in 2007) and Scotland (in 2013), the development of a Global Network on Teaching Quality and Effectiveness (in 2012), and the focus on teacher quality of The Global Cities Education Network, are examples of international attempts to address the attraction, education, development, retention, and evaluation of teachers. The *No Child Left Behind Act* mandated that teachers receive high quality professional learning opportunities that were: sustained; aligned with imposed standards; focused on increasing knowledge of their subject and of scientifically-based instructional strategies; and regularly evaluated for effectiveness on teachers and students. The more recent *Every Student Succeeds Act* (ESSA, 2015)—which replaced *No Child Left Behind* after it was widely recognised as being unsuccessful—outlines supporting educator development by providing teachers, principals, and other school leaders with professional development activities that are evidence-based and address literacy, numeracy, or remedial needs.

A highly influential McKinsey and Company report (Barber & Mourshed, 2007) presents the argument that in order to improve instruction, individual teachers need to become aware of specific weaknesses in their own practice; understand what they do and why they do it; deliver instruction in an effective and efficient manner; gain understanding of 'best practices'; and be motivated to make the necessary improvement, usually incentivised by a shared sense of purpose and drive to make a difference. This McKinsey and Company report has been used to justify education reform around the world, but has been criticised for being methodologically flawed, selective, superficial, implausible, and based on a thin evidence base (Coffield, 2012). Frank Coffield (2012) notes that the report is the work of policy analysts who are removed from both the complexities of classrooms and from nuanced, critical research. He asserts that they espouse a high performance model of schooling highly prescriptive, top down, and mechanistic, and promote a notion of teaching and learning that is narrowly conceived and technocratic. In this model, "teachers are reduced to the status of technicians, of agents of the state who 'deliver' the ideas of others" (Coffield, 2012, p. 145). The professional autonomy and agency of teachers and school leaders is undermined, and policy decisions are made based on oversimplified, limited, and limiting reports of evidence.

The Australian context in which I operate also provides examples of system level attempts to develop 'high quality teachers' and excellence in teaching. The *Melbourne Declaration on Educational Goals for Young Australians* (Barr et al., 2008) outlined the goal for the Australian education system of developing high quality teachers to improve student learning. The NAPLAN standardised testing regime was introduced in the same year, with the aim of measuring student achievement in order to drive education improvement. In 2010 the Australian government created the MySchool website, which publishes school NAPLAN results online, thereby giving parents and communities the ability to judge and compare schools according to their NAPLAN performance. The MySchool online tool compares 'like schools' according to a socio-educational advantage index. In the meantime, the National Partnership Agreement for Improving Teacher Quality was signed and rolled out, which committed to developing teacher professional standards.

The establishment of the Australian Institute for Teaching and School Leadership (AITSL) in 2010 was soon followed by the release of national professional standards; the Australian Professional Standards for Teachers were introduced in 2010, and Standards for Principals were introduced in 2011. The Australian government trialled reforms such as performance based teacher pay that rewards quality teaching, while the Australian Review of Funding for Schooling (Gonski et al., 2011), the National Plan for School Improvement (Commonwealth of Australia, 2013), and the report of the Review to Achieve Educational Excellence in Australian Schools (Gonski et al., 2018) all positioned teacher quality as fundamental to improving education for Australia's students. Greg Craven et al.'s (2014) report for the Teacher Education Ministerial Advisory Group (TEMAG) states that "the evidence is clear: enhancing the capability of teachers is vital to raising the overall quality of Australia's school system and lifting student outcomes" (p. viii). The recent review of teacher registration in Australia (AITSL, 2018) holds "improving and reinforcing teacher quality" as its number one key area of focus. The review states that "the continued focus on the performance and development of fully registered teachers is critical to drive quality and improve student outcomes" (p. iii). These reports, agreements, and reforms continue to propel the teacher quality agenda in Australia, and fuel the ongoing search for the best ways to help teachers improve their teaching. As Glenn Savage and Bob Lingard (2018) have pointed out, these reforms position teacher quality as a central issue facing Australian schooling, with additional federal funding conditional upon jurisdictions working towards national aims.

The focus on teacher quality is solidifying and snowballing as time goes on. It shows no signs of abating. The global push to develop the 'quality' of teachers and teaching has gone hand in hand with the notion of holding teachers and schools to account over performance data through endless processes of quality assurance (Groundwater-Smith & Mockler, 2009). Data, accountabilities, and cultures of compliance become the accepted realities around which teachers and school leaders define themselves, while the humanity, complexity, and voices of students, teachers, and school leaders are stifled and disregarded (Ball, 2016; Keddie, 2017). As professional learning has been identified as something that raises student achievement by developing teachers, it has become a focus of governments, districts, and schools around the world. The danger is that professional learning becomes subsumed by this accountability culture that is hyper focused on questionable measures, invalid comparisons, and what can be easily counted rather than what has the potential to lead to positive and lasting transformation.

What's in this book

This book is based in my own trust in the teaching profession, and my advocacy for policymakers and others to listen to those actually in our classrooms and schools (Netolicky, 2019). This book is not about fixing teachers but about empowerment and meaningful learning. In it I ask: What is it that really changes what teachers believe and what we do, for the benefits of our students, ourselves, and our communities?

This Introduction sets the context for this book by outlining the agendas around the education world that are propelling professional learning budgets, decisions, and interventions. It makes the case that professional learning is indeed important, but argues that the focus should be on trusting and growing teachers and the teaching profession, not on visible performance measures and competition.

In the chapters that follow this Introduction, I tease out the field of professional learning by reviewing and synthesising research literature, as well as exploring why professional learning is important, what kinds of professional learning are beneficial, and explicating what theory can look like in practice. This structure, that draws research and practice together, means that the tone in this book moves between the more formal academic tone of a literature review, and the more personal voice of my own experiences. Such is the multiplicity of identities, and the constant code-switching of the pracademic author. The writing in this book reflects the way I think and work: look to the literature, consider research (often in systematic, detached, evidence-informed ways), and then consider contexts and lived experiences (often in more intuitive, subjective, experienced-informed ways). Each of Chapters 1 to 8 ends with a list of key takeaways, briefly encapsulating the messages of that chapter.

Chapter 1 defines transformational professional learning as that which actively changes a person's ways of knowing, thinking, and doing, leading to changes in practice. It sets up the notion of transformation—and the shaping of beliefs and practices—as a useful frame for considering professional learning. Chapter 1 additionally explores research literature around professional learning, including the trends and gaps in this broad and contested field.

Chapters 2, 3, 4, 5, and 6 are each about a particular kind of professional learning. Each is structured with an introduction, including definition and research literature. This is followed by a 'spotlight on research' (around what my PhD said about that phenomenon) and a 'spotlight on practice' (in which I explore my own practitioner experiences around that phenomenon and what it looks like when it is living and breathing in the lives of educators and schools) in each chapter.

Chapter 2 is about what we might think of as traditional professional learning. It explores those things often advertised as 'PD' such as speakers, courses, and conferences, and finds that these have their place within the professional learning landscape, providing content learning, time for thinking, and opportunities for networking and professional conversation.

Chapter 3 emerges from one of my PhD findings: that teachers and school leaders professionally learn in a wide variety of contexts, at sometimes surprising times, and in sometimes unexpected places. This chapter questions assumptions that professional learning only happens in work time, or in designated learning places. Professional learning, it argues, happens in scenarios that are professional and personal, formal and informal, in and out of educational contexts, and singular and collaborative.

Perhaps the heart of the book, Chapter 4 reviews literature on informal and formal collaborative professional learning. This includes technical approaches such as professional learning communities and lesson study, but also relational and cultural ways to think about professional collaboration. Collaborative professional learning needs to be deliberately designed with a clear shared focus on improving outcomes for students and transparent norms, protocols, processes, and data analysis. It should also facilitate graceful disagreement, productive conflict, collect-ive responsibility, and peer accountability. The chapter shows that professional collaboration can benefit students and teachers, and explores to what extent collaboration within schools needs to be harmonious or challenging.

Chapter 5 shares clear definitions of, and teases out the differences between, mentoring and coaching. It has a particular focus on coaching as a site of profes-sional learning. The three-year strategic project I led—the piloting and implementa-tion of a model for professional learning involving lesson observation and coaching—provides a case study of how coaching can be used as professional learning within a school.

Chapter 6 explores self-directed learning, including the terms *self-directed learn-ing, andragogy*, and *heutagogy*. It delves into the role of social media such as Twit-ter for 'do it yourself' learning and discusses the findings in this emerging area of professional learning.

Chapter 7 considers the role in professional learning of professional standards, and the ongoing tension between professionalism and evaluation. While profes-sional standards are often seen as a policy mechanism intended to assess and improve teacher quality, they can be reclaimed by teachers and schools as a formative tool to frame meaningful reflection on and discussions about practice.

Chapter 8 examines the kind of leadership and school conditions required for effective leadership of professional learning. This chapter encourages the consider-ation of alternate ways of leading beyond well-worn archetypes; judicious use of evidence to inform decision making around professional learning; and leadership by teachers and middle leaders, as well as senior leaders and the principal. It warns against uncritical compliance to accountability measures and encourages resistance to oversimplified professional learning solutions that promote a potentially limiting 'what works' approach.

The Conclusion explores the answer to the question: *So what?* It draws the book's themes together and teases out the implications of this book's argument. It outlines final thoughts about how teachers, school leaders, scholars, and policymakers can and should think about professional learning.

About the 'spotlight on research'

The 'spotlight on research' sections of this book move beyond the overview of research presented at the beginning of each chapter. They shine a spotlight on my PhD research and what it found about professional learning. The data and findings explored here complement the broader research cited in each chapter. I enrolled in my PhD in October 2012. At the time there was a deafening global push for better teaching and better student achievement. Education systems and schools had their eyes firmly on standardised test scores. As discussed above, the terms *teacher quality, quality teaching* and *teaching effectiveness* were being used to denote the quality of teachers' teaching, in terms of its effectiveness in adding value to student learning, as measured by standardised, often high-stakes, tests. There were resulting impacts on education policy and practice, with new teacher evaluation systems being rolled out across the USA, talk of performance based pay for teachers, and initiatives in professional development around the world promising to make teachers and their teaching better. The 2011 release of the Australian Professional Standards for Teachers was intended to improve and assess teaching. Around the world, the media were reporting on global education rankings based on tests such as PISA. Who was at the top, they asked? Who was lagging behind or falling behind? Government rhetoric spoke of standards, rigour, and world-class education. Teachers were increasingly being described as in deficit and in need of fixing.

Within this global milieu, as a teacher and school leader myself, my PhD study sought to understand two things:

1.   The role of professional learning on identities and professional growth; and
2.   What professional learning was transformational for participants.

That is, while schools and education systems were spending enormous amounts of money on professional learning, what actually made a difference? I looked within my own school context to find out what I could, interviewing teachers and school leaders who were involved in a then-newly-introduced school-based model of professional learning that involved lesson observation data and cognitive coaching. The 2013 commencement of this model—that in my PhD I call the *Teacher Growth Initiative*, and that in this book I will call the *coaching intervention*—provided a unique time and place against which to set a study of professional learning. I did not, however, just ask participants about their experience of the intervention. Rather, I asked broader questions about participants' lifelong learning experiences.

The spotlights on research are based in Australia, as I share the perspectives and voices of myself (as researcher and embedded participant) and the other 13 participants of my PhD study, as eked out via interviews. The interviewed participants were two teachers, six middle leaders, and five executive leaders from one independent Australian school. In fact, four teachers were interviewed for this study, but—perhaps indicative of the constraints and professional vulnerabilities facing teachers—two teachers withdrew from my study after the interviews were completed and transcribed and so their data were unable to be interpreted.

The teachers were interviewed twice by an independent interviewer in the first pilot year of the intervention (2013), while the leaders were interviewed once by me in the second pilot year (2014). I was in fact more than the embedded researcher observer in this research. As the leader of the coaching intervention, I was interviewed, using the same external interviewer, interview protocols, and interview timelines, as the teachers. The use of an external interviewer for the teachers in this study was a condition of the ethics board in order to protect participants. I briefed the interviewer on the interview questions and protocols, which were then applied to interviews of the teachers and I. The teacher data I was able to interpret were transcripts of the interviews after they had been de-identified and authenticated by participants. This ethical protection was not required for the interviews of me and the school leaders.

Interview was a research method that allowed me to delve deeply into the stories and experiences of these teachers and school leaders. Open-ended questions, and plenty of paraphrasing and probing questions, allowed me to encourage participants to think aloud about their beliefs and experiences. My study was conducted with the intention of honouring and capturing the essence of the stories and voices of teacher and school leader participants. The spotlights on research throughout this book draw direct quotations from my PhD interview data, allowing those voices to shine through. At times in this book I share quotes from the interviews of myself. While it seems strange to quote myself, these words capture my thinking at those moments in time, in the context of the studied coaching intervention.

Drawing on my PhD study allows me to offer and lift up voices from the field—rather than those of the Minister's office, think tank, or academe—and bring them together with research and scholarship. In doing so it embodies a yoking of praxis (the wisdom of practice) and research, and argues for approaches to professional learning driven by both what academic scholarship can tell us, and by a deep trust in the wisdom of the teaching profession. The data and findings of my PhD are of course limited, but they act as a keyhole into the realities of teachers and school leaders, and a microcosm of what teachers and school leaders perceive to be transformational professional learning. My PhD study illuminates a facet of how school-based professional learning-in-context impacts on professional identity and makes deeply transformational learning possible.

More information about the study and its method is included at the end of this book as Appendix A. I have also written about methodological complexities and ethical decision making (Netolicky & Barnes, 2018). Of course, the full 300-page dissertation (Netolicky, 2016) is available online to download if you are interested to read more.

About the 'spotlight on practice'

The 'spotlight on practice' sections of this book draw upon my practitioner experience as a teacher and school leader. They discuss professional learning, in practice, from my perspective as an educator embedded in that practice. Some offer examples of school-based interventions in which I have been involved. Others present reflections on my personal experiences. The school-based examples of practice come from my roles as a teacher, middle leader, and senior leader in schools in the last 20 years. These include as teacher of English and Literature, head of English faculties; director of a coaching intervention to improve professional culture and teaching practice; head of professional learning; and part of a senior leadership team charged with staff development, reward, and performance review. My experiences of school leadership, as well as those of my participants in the spotlight on research sections, are particularly important, as these are experiences so rarely seen in research, policy, and media discourses, where there is seldom a focus on teacher or middle leadership.

Personal experiences in the spotlights on practice draw from my experience of being a coach and being coached; of being simultaneously a parent and a teacher; of being a PhD candidate while also working in a school and parenting my then-pre-school-age children. These vignettes of practice provide examples of how research literature around professional learning can be brought to life in schools and in the lives of those working in schools.

References

Australian Institute for Teaching and School Leadership (AITSL). (2018). *One teaching profession: Teacher registration in Australia*. Carlton South: Education Council.

Baguley, M., & Kerby, M. (2012). Teachers' perceptions of professional development and the role of the university. In P. A. Danaher, L. De George-Walker, R. Henderson, K. J. Matthews, W. Midgeley, K. Noble, M. A. Tyler, & C. H. Arden (Eds.). *Constructing capacities: Building capabilities through learning and engagement* (pp. 107–123). Newcastle upon Tyne: Cambridge Scholars.

Ball, S. J. (2016). Subjectivity as a site of struggle: Refusing neoliberalism? *British Journal of Sociology of Education, 37*(8), 1129–1146.

Ball, S. J. (2017). *The education debate* (3rd ed.). Bristol: Policy Press.

Barber, M., & Mourshed, M. (2007). *How the world's best performing schools come out on top*. McKinsey and Company.

Barr, A., Gillard, J., Firth, V., Scrymgour, M., Welford, R., Lomax-Smith, J., … Constable, E. (2008). *Melbourne declaration on educational goals for young Australians*. Carlton, Australia: Ministerial Council on Education, Employment, Training and Youth Affairs.

Burstow, B. (2018). *Effective teacher development: Theory and practice in professional learning*. London: Bloomsbury.

Call, K. (2018). Professional teaching standards: A comparative analysis of their history, implementation and efficacy. *Australian Journal of Teacher Education, 43*(3), 6.

Coffield, F. (2012). Why the McKinsey reports will not improve school systems. *Journal of Education Policy, 27*(1), 131–149.

Commonwealth of Australia. (2013). *National plan for school improvement*. Canberra: Commonwealth of Australia.

Congress, US. (2001). No Child Left Behind Act of 2001. *Public Law, 107*, 110.

Connell, R. (2009). Good teachers on dangerous ground: Towards a new view of teacher quality and professionalism. *Critical Studies in Education, 50*(3), 213–229.

Cordingley, P. (2015). The contribution of research to teachers' professional learning and development. *Oxford Review of Education*, *41*(2), 234–252.

Craven, G., Beswick, K., Fleming, J., Fletcher, T., Green, M., Jensen, B., Leinonen, E., & Ricjards, F. (2014). *Action now: Classroom ready teachers*. Teacher Education Ministerial Advisory Group.

Crehan, L. (2016). *Cleverlands: The secrets behind the success of the world's education superpowers*. London: Unbound.

Darling-Hammond, L., Wei, R. C., Andree, A., Richardson, N., & Orphanos, S. (2009). *Professional learning in the learning profession: A status report on teacher development in the U.S. and abroad*. Technical Report. Stanford: National Staff Development Council.

Department of Education. England. (2010). *The importance of teaching: The schools white paper*. London: The Stationery Office.

Desimone, L. M. (2009). Improving impact studies of teachers' professional development: Toward better conceptualisations and measures. *Educational Researcher*, *38*(3), 181–199.

Desimone, L. M., Porter, A. C., Garet, M. S., Yoon, K. S., & Birman, B. F. (2002). Effects of professional development on teachers' instruction: Results from a three-year longitudinal study. *Educational Evaluation and Policy Analysis*, *24*(2), 81–112.

Drago-Severson, E. (2009). *Leading adult learning: Supporting adult development in our schools*. Thousand Oaks: Corwin.

Drago-Severson, E. (2012). *Helping educators grow: Strategies and practices for leadership development*. Cambridge: Harvard Education.

Drago-Severson, E., & Blum-DeStefano, J. (2018). *Leading change together: Developing educator capacity within schools and systems*. Alexandria: ASCD.

Every Student Succeeds Act. (2015). *Every Student Succeeds Act (ESSA): A comprehensive guide*. Washington DC: US Department of Education.

Fullan, M. (2011). Choosing the wrong drivers for whole school reform. *Seminar Series*, 204.

Gonski, D., Arcus, T., Boston, K., Gould, V., Johnson, W., O'Brien, L., … Roberts, M. (2018). *Through growth to achievement: The report of the review to achieve educational excellence in Australian schools*. Canberra: Commonwealth of Australia.

Gonski, D., Boston, K., Greiner, K., Lawrence, C., Scales, B., & Tannock, P. (2011). *Review of funding for schooling: Final report*. Canberra: Department of Education, Employment and Workplace Relations.

Groundwater-Smith, S., & Mockler, N. (2009). *Teacher professional learning in an age of compliance: Mind the gap*. Dordrecht: Springer.

Keddie, A. (2017). School autonomy reform and public education in Australia: Implications for social justice. *The Australian Educational Researcher*, *44*(4-5), 373–390.

Korthagen, F. (2017). Inconvenient truths about teacher learning: Towards professional development 3.0. *Teachers and Teaching*, *23*(4), 387–405.

Leigh, A. (2010). Estimating teacher effectiveness from two-year changes in students' test scores. *Economics of Education Review*, *29*(3), 480–488.

Lewis, S., & Hogan, A. (2016). Reform first and ask questions later? The implications of (fast) schooling policy and 'silver bullet' solutions. *Critical Studies in Education*, *60*(1), 1–18.

Lingard, B., Thompson, G., & Sellar, S. (2016). National testing from an Australian perspective. In B. Lingard, G. Thompson, & S. Sellar (Eds.). *National testing in schools: An Australian assessment* (pp. 1–17). Abingdon: Routledge.

Mockler, N. (2013). Teacher professional learning in a neoliberal age: Audit, professionalism and identity. *Australian Journal of Teacher Education*, *38*(10), 35–47.

Netolicky, D. M. (2016). *Down the rabbit hole: Professional identities, professional learning, and change in one Australian school* (Doctoral dissertation, Murdoch University).

Netolicky, D. M. (2019). Elevating the professional identities and voices of teachers and school leaders in educational research, practice, and policymaking. In D. M. Netolicky, J. Andrews, &

C. Paterson (Eds.). *Flip the system Australia: What matters in education* (pp. 9–18). Abingdon: Routledge.

Netolicky, D. M., Andrews, J., & Paterson, C. (Eds.). (2019). *Flip the system Australia: What matters in education*. Abingdon: Routledge.

Netolicky, D. M., & Barnes, N. (2018). Method as a journey: A narrative dialogic partnership illuminating decision-making in qualitative educational research. *International Journal of Research & Method in Education, 41*(5), 500–513.

O'Hanlon, C. (1996). Is there a difference between action research and quality development? Within or beyond the constraints?. In C. O'Hanlon (Ed.). *Professional development through action research in educational settings* (pp. 73–88). London: Routledge Falmer.

Organisation for Economic Cooperation and Development (OECD). (2010). *PISA 2009 results: What students know and can do* – student performance in reading, mathematics and science (Volume I) http://dx.doi.org/10.1787/9789264091450-en.

Savage, G. C., & Lingard, B. (2018). Changing modes of governance in Australian teacher education policy. In N. Hobbel & B. L. Bales (Eds.). *Navigating the common good in teacher education policy: Critical and international perspectives* (pp. 74–90). New York: Routledge.

Sellar, S., Thompson, G., & Rutkowski, D. (2017). *The global education race: Taking the measure of PISA and international testing*. Calgary: Brush Education.

Stevenson, H. (2019). Editorial: Professional learning – What is the point? *Professional Development in Education, 45*(1), 1–2.

Thompson, G., Adie, L., & Klenowski, V. (2018). Validity and participation: Implications for school comparison of Australia's National Assessment Program. *Journal of Education Policy, 33*(6), 759–777.

Timperley, H., Wilson, A., Barrar, H., & Fung, I. (2007). *Teacher professional learning and development: Best evidence synthesis iteration*. Wellington: New Zealand Ministry for Education.

van Kuijk, M. F., Deunk, M. I., Bosker, R. J., & Ritzema, E. S. (2016). Goals, data use, and instruction: The effect of a teacher professional development program on reading achievement. *School Effectiveness and School Improvement, 27*(2), 135–156.

Waite, D. (2016). Of charlatans, sorcerers, alchemists, demagogues, profit-mongers, tyrants and kings: Educational reform and the death by a thousand cuts. *The Urban Review, 48*(1), 123–148.

Wiliam, D. (2016). *Leadership for teacher learning: Creating a culture where all teachers improve so that all students succeed*. Moorabbin: Hawker Brownlow Education.

Wiliam, D. (2018). *Creating the schools our children need: Why what we're doing now won't help much (and what we can do instead)*. Palm Beach: Learning Sciences.

Yoon, K. S., Duncan, T., Lee, S. W.-Y., Scarloss, B., & Shapley, K. (2007). *Reviewing the evidence on how teacher professional development affects student achievement (Issues & Answers Report, REL 2007–No. 033)*. Washington DC: U.S. Department of Education, Institute of Education Sciences, National Centre for Education Evaluation and Regional Assistance, Regional Educational Laboratory Southwest.

Zammit, K., Sinclair, C., Cole, B., Singh, M., Costley, D., Brown a'Court, L., & Rushton, K. (2007). *Teaching and leading for quality Australian schools: A review and synthesis of research-based knowledge*. Sydney: University of Western Sydney for Teaching Australia.

Chapter 1

Transformational professional learning

Around the world, teachers and school leaders are expected to professionally learn, and to be constantly committed to their professional development. Despite the acknowledged importance of professional learning, however, there are inequitable opportunities for professional learning, and approaches inconsistent with what is likely to have a positive impact on teachers and consequently students. In the USA many teachers do not have access to effective professional development (Darling-Hammond et al., 2009). The professional learning to which they do have access is often too short in duration to make a difference to knowledge or practice (Darling-Hammond et al., 2009). In Canada there are also uneven opportunities for professional learning across the education system (Campbell et al., 2017). In Australia, the report known colloquially as 'Gonski 2.0,' and more lengthily titled *Through growth to achievement: Report of the review to achieve educational excellence in Australian schools* (Gonski et al., 2018), outlines what research literature has been saying for some time: that teachers need to meaningfully collaborate, and that schools need to provide growth-focused professional learning environments in which teachers can interrogate and improve their practice, based on knowing research and knowing their students.

This chapter defines transformational professional learning and sets up the notions of transformation—via the shaping of professional beliefs and practices—as a useful frame for considering professional learning. It connects professional learning with identity and explores research literature around professional learning, including the trends, gaps, and cautions in this broad and contested field. In this way it provides a theoretical lens through which to view the professional learning approaches explored in Chapters 2 to 6.

Defining transformational professional learning

The focus on professional learning to improve teaching and learning points to crucial questions. How, why, and when do educators learn and grow? What learning leads educators to shift their teaching and leading beliefs and practices? As I noted in the Introduction, this book is concerned with effective professional learning, and more specifically *transformational professional learning* (not to be confused with Jack Mezirow's *transformative learning theory*). So much in education promises to *transform*. Transformation implies change and that learning can be more than the acquisition of knowledge and skills (Illeris, 2014). *Transformational* is a seductive term that promises much, but is often used emptily.

For the purpose of this book, an understanding of the word 'transformational,' in the context of professional learning, is key, providing the basis for a particular view of professional learning: one concerned with those experiences and processes that have an impact on what teachers and school leaders think, believe, feel, and do.

To tease out and clarify my meaning, here I draw on Ellie Drago-Severson's (2009) description of adult learning as being *informational*, increasing knowledge and skills, or *transformational*, actively changing how a person knows through shifts in cognition, emotion, and capacity (Drago-Severson & Blum-DeStefano, 2018). While increasing knowledge and skills is important for the teaching profession, better knowledge and skills do not always change or improve practice. Someone might tell us an apparently better way of doing something, but unless we believe in a reason for a change, knowing a different way of doing something is unlikely to ensure that teachers or leaders change ingrained habits. Transformational learning shapes and re-forms the internal fabric of a person's knowing, doing, being, and becoming. It creates shifts in knowledge, practice, or identity (Mockler, 2013). Transformational learning is about meaning making and is therefore tied to the notion of identity. It acknowledges that professional learning is connected to how individuals perceive, imagine, and enact their selves. Teachers learn in communities that enable them to develop: a vision for their practice; understandings about teaching, learning, and children; dispositions about how to use this knowledge; practices that allow them to enact their intentions and beliefs; and tools that support their efforts (Darling-Hammond et al., 2009). This kind of professional learning shifts educator professional learning from a focus on disseminating information to harnessing what is known about how people learn (Muijs et al., 2014), and what kind of learning actually influences beliefs and behaviour.

My definition of transformational professional learning is as follows.

Transformational professional learning shifts beliefs, and thereby behaviours, of professionals. It is tied to an individual's personal and professional identity.

Unless their existing beliefs are engaged, teachers are likely to reject ideas that conflict with their current thinking, dismissing them as unrealistic or inappropriate to their own contexts (Timperley, 2008). Beliefs tend to change before practice, although sometimes being asked to do something practical (putting practice first) can change beliefs, if our experience of the outcomes of that practice shift our beliefs. A change in beliefs means a change in identity, in how we see and describe ourselves as professionals, as teachers, as leaders.

In the Preface to their edited collection on the transformational learning experiences of counsellors, Michelle Shuler, Elizabeth Keller-Dupree, and Katrina Cook (2017) explain that:

> We can all likely identify that moment in life when real learning took place. Not just content learning, but real, applicable, feel-it-in-our-gut learning, that moved us to a deeper understanding of ourselves and others. These moments unearth our process, they profoundly impact us, and they shape who we are continually becoming. It is this type of learning that

transforms our knowledge into deeply relevant experiences. It is in these moments that our personal self and our professional self intersect (p.vii).

Transformational learning involves moving the learner to a deeper understanding of self and other, and having a profound impact on the self (Shuler et al., 2017). The personal and professional self is inextricably connected.

So, transformational professional learning is learning that shifts cognition, emotion, and capacity. It is learning that changes teacher and school leader beliefs in order to change the macro and micro decisions that teachers make in their practice. It is personal as well as professional. It is human and complex.

The role of identity

Transformational learning is deeply connected with the notion of *identity*. As educators, our narratives of self-identity are essential for our professional growth. Nicole Mockler (2013) argues that, in discussions of professional learning for educators, using a lens of identity is more useful than one of teacher quality. It means looking at who people are rather than how they perform. However, the body of scholarship on teacher professional identity has been called an under-developed and confused field (Bridges et al., 2012) limited to primarily trad-itional routes to becoming a teacher and traditional classroom experiences, leaving out those involved in alternative routes such as fast-track teacher training (Thomas & Mockler, 2018). It is often focused on the teacher, sometimes on the principal, and rarely on the middle leader.

The term *identity* needs teasing out, as it is a slippery concept (Lawler, 2014) lacking a clear definition (Mockler, 2011). Those writing about and researching professional identity can embrace the complexity of identity's many intercon-nected facets, but should aim for precision in their explanations of their approaches (Lawler, 2014). Some researchers support the notion that professional identities are fixed or formed early, but much research demonstrates that iden-tities are flexible, multiple, and continually shaped by contexts and relationships. Not only do identities shift, but they are multifaceted and situation-specific. That is, each of us has a fluid and ever-changing set of identities (Netolicky, 2019). We call into action the identity appropriate to the situation in which we are currently functioning. This book aligns with theorists who conceptualise identities as pluralistic, multiple, overlapping, and intersecting constructions, operated by the individual and changing over time (Holland et al., 1998; Lawler, 2014). Within this frame, professional identities are fluid amalgams that are profoundly linked to practice.

For the purpose of this book, my definition of identity is as follows.

Identity is the situated, ongoing process through which we make sense of ourselves, to ourselves and to others.

That is, identity is continual and changing, not fixed. It is a process, not a product. It is embedded in social, organisational, and economic contexts. It is about making sense of ourselves in the worlds in which we live, and is operated by the individual. Here I draw on Dorothy Holland et al.'s (1998) description of identities as "imaginings of self in worlds of action" (p. 5), and Sue Lasky's

(2005) argument that identities are how teachers define themselves to themselves and to others. We are never finished, never foreclose on an identity, but fluidly negotiate our self-perceptions in a variety of contexts. We imagine and enact our identities by negotiating and reimaging our past, present, and potential future selves. Professional growth is ongoing and we are always becoming; becoming who we are, what we believe, and how we operate.

Identities are simultaneously individual and collaborative. We construct our versions of ourselves based on our relationships with others, with organisations, and with contexts. The connection between self and context is what Laura Desimone (2009) talks about when she outlines the concept of *coherence* in professional learning. That is, the extent to which teacher learning is consistent with the teacher's knowledge and beliefs, and also the extent to which professional learning is consistent with education policies and reforms.

Teachers and school leaders need to feel a sense of ideological 'fit' with their schools and education systems. Individuals want to identify with the collective identity.

In my PhD study, the teacher and leader participants showed the desire to align with a team or organisation's identity and were attracted to its purpose. While Peter Gronn (2003) suggests that individuals rework their perspectives in relation to their contexts, my PhD study (Netolicky, 2016a) found that, while context affects professional identity, individuals also choose their contexts to fit their individual identities. That is, contexts shape individuals, individuals shape contexts, and individuals can choose contexts with which they feel an identity fit, or leave contexts in which they feel they do not fit. A sense of belonging and self-authenticity was important. My PhD participants indicated that they stayed in schools that resonated with their senses of professional self, and left schools in which they did not feel aligned with organisational purpose and action. All of the participants in my study expressed the need for a sense of fit between individual professional identity and the school context. This suggests that school-based interventions, including professional learning, should carefully consider how to harness identities and internal purpose. Schools need to be clear, consistent, and communicative about their organisational identities, including values and purpose, thereby allowing staff to connect and 'fit.'

Unfortunately, in today's education world of hyper accountability, surveillance, and limiting standards, educators' identities are often reduced down to a limited and limiting range of options. Those things at the core of learning that transform cognition and identity—critical reflection, dialogue with self and others, awareness of context, and authentic relationships (Illeris, 2014)—are often put in the 'too hard' or the 'we'd love to but we don't have the time' basket by teachers, school leaders, and schools. This book acts as a reminder to systems, schools, and those working in schools, that transformational learning should be a priority, for the learning of our students, but also for the wellbeing, energy, motivation, and cohesive experience of our teachers and school leaders. Those designing and implementing professional learning reforms would benefit from engaging with teacher and school leader identities, with the whole person, and all the entwined personal and professional complexity that entails. Considering professional identity alongside professional learning allows for the exploration of what it is that shapes educators' development of professional identity perceptions, what shifts those self-perceptions, and in what ways schools and systems might work with a greater understanding of educator identities when designing and implementing professional learning.

Pursuing transformational professional learning that engages with educators' identities, beliefs, and emotions, as well as their cognition, leads to learning-enriched schools like those described by Susan Rosenholtz (1991) in which "an abundant spirit of continuous improvement" seems to "hover school-wide, because no one ever stopped learning to teach" (p. 208). She describes educators in effective schools as "clumped together in a critical mass, like uranium fuel rods in a reactor" (p. 208), illustrating school communities as hubs of continuous collaborative learning in which individuals work alongside one another for a common purpose. It is worth considering, from the perspectives of teachers and school leaders themselves, what changes their beliefs in order for them to embrace education reform or reshape their professional practices.

What research says about professional learning

Professional learning is a heavily-researched area in the field of education. There is so much written about professional learning for teachers that it can seem like there is a confusing overload of information. Among all this research, trends have emerged on what constitutes meaningful learning for teachers. Carol Campbell et al. (2017), in their review of professional learning literature, identified effective professional learning as evidence-informed, with a balance of teacher voice and system coherence. Teachers in Joanne Wong and Alfredo Bautista's (2018) study identified three types of professional learning: *formal* (facilitator-directed); *informal* (teacher-led); and *individual* (self-directed). Derek Glover and Sue Law (1996) identify four kinds of professional learning. These include that which fulfils:

- *Individual* professional needs, such as the knowledge and skills to teach effectively;
- *Departmental, year, or group* needs, focused on developing team approaches and sharing expertise;
- *Whole school* needs, based on organisational values and goals; and
- *Multi-institutional* needs, where groups of schools or networks of teachers come together for professional learning.

Effective professional development can positively affect teacher attitudes and skills (Elliott, 2017), and can influence the beliefs of teachers (Borg, 2011). While teacher beliefs have been found to be instrumental in shaping teachers' practice, they have also been found to be resistant to attempts by teacher educators and policymakers to change them (Priestley et al., 2015). That is, once we think we know what works for our students and staff, it is hard to change our minds. Models of professional learning that seek to impose a generic solution on teachers and schools, do not take into account the individual differences between individuals and contexts. For professional learning to be effective, it needs to be relevant, address identified needs, lead to a change in teacher knowledge and understanding, influence teacher practice, and lead to improved outcomes for learners (AITSL, 2018); supporting teachers to reflect on, question, and consciously improve their practice (AITSL, 2012).

Research identifies particular content foci for professional learning:

- Professional learning that focuses on *content knowledge* (Campbell et al., 2017; Darling-Hammond et al., 2009; Desimone, 2009).
- Professional learning that focuses on *how students learn and how to teach them* (Campbell et al., 2017; Desimone, 2009).
- Professional learning *connected to other school initiatives* (Darling-Hammond et al., 2009) and *consistent with wider policy trends* (Timperley et al., 2007). Helen Timperley et al. (2007) in their best evidence synthesis of 97 individual studies and groups of studies around how to promote teacher learning in ways that impact on outcomes for students, identify the need for a balance of school-based initiatives led by school leaders, and engaging external expertise to support those working within a school.

Research also identifies what kinds of experiences of professional learning are effective:

- Professional learning that is *ongoing* in duration (Campbell et al., 2017; Desimone, 2009; Hargreaves & Fullan, 2012). Laura Desimone (2009) advocates specifically for ongoing professional learning that has a duration of 20 hours or more over time.
- Professional learning in which the *individual has some control* over their own learning (Campbell et al., 2017; Wiliam, 2016).
- Professional learning that is *active* and *variable* (Campbell et al., 2017; Desimone, 2009).
- Professional learning that is *job-embedded* (Campbell et al., 2017; Lieberman et al., 2017; Zepeda, 2013). Sally Zepeda (2013) describes job-embedded learning as occurring in the context of the work setting, relating to specific work experiences, and involving ongoing discussion and sharing with colleagues. Much learning in workplace contexts is embedded in daily work.

The focus on collaboration in teacher learning is based on the argument that teacher learning experiences should build strong working relationships among teachers (Darling-Hammond et al., 2009) and provide opportunities to interact within a community of professionals (Timperley et al., 2007). Laura Desimone (2009) specifies activities such as observing expert teachers, being observed, reviewing student work, and leading discussions. For her, collective participation should be not only within schools, but also across schools. Scholars suggest models of teacher professional learning that are collaborative and teacher-led, rather than individual or top down. Professional learning supported by research literature includes the following approaches:

- *Professional learning communities*, explained in Chapter 4;
- Teacher collaboration around lesson observations, including *instructional rounds, quality teaching rounds* and *lesson study*, some of which are explored in more detail in Chapter 4;
- *Mentoring* and *coaching*, teased out in Chapter 5.

There are additionally calls to develop schools as social and relational places of solidarity and entrenched collaboration (Hargreaves & Fullan, 2012; Hargreaves & O'Connor, 2018). This means going beyond the procedural mechanics to culture and the ways in which teachers and school leaders interact. It means developing coherent, collaborative context-specific understandings of 'how we do things around here' that are embedded and enacted by colleagues each and every day.

The above approaches to professional learning are consistent with the Australian Gonski 2.0 report's (Gonski et al., 2018) singling out of the following modes of teacher collaboration as particularly effective: peer observation and feedback, coaching, mentoring, team teaching, and joint research projects. The above approaches are also consistent with the standards for professional learning released in 2011 by the USA's National Staff Development Council (now called Learning Forward). Those standards (Learning Forward, 2011) are as follows. Professional learning that increases educator effectiveness and results for all students:

- Occurs within learning communities committed to continuous improvement, collective responsibility, and goal alignment.
- Increases educator effectiveness and results for all students requires prioritising, monitoring, and coordinating resources for educator learning.
- Integrates theories, research, and models of human learning to achieve its intended outcomes.
- Aligns its outcomes with educator performance and student curriculum standards.
- Requires skilful leadership by leaders who develop capacity, advocate, and create support systems for professional learning.
- Uses a variety of sources and types of student, educator, and system data to plan, assess, and evaluate professional learning.
- Applies research on change and sustains support for implementation of professional learning for long term change.

The above standards show that it is not only the content and type of professional learning that schools and systems need to consider. Time and money are crucial considerations in professional learning; it needs to be supported and resourced by schools (Wiliam, 2016). Timperley et al. (2007) found that providing sufficient time for extended learning opportunities was vital to the success of professional learning. Meanwhile, the 2012 Californian Task Force on Educator Excellence report argued that a consistent share of education budgets be dedicated to professional learning investments (Darling-Hammond & Steinhauser, 2012). Campbell et al. (2017) also say that for professional learning to be effective, it needs resources, external support, and supportive and engaged leadership. Teachers need time and space for both professional collaboration and to visit each other's classrooms to observe alternate ways of engaging with subject matter, ascertaining and measuring student achievement, and utilising a diversity of teaching strategies (Fleming & Kleinhenz, 2007).

What teachers want from professional learning

Research can tell us what kinds of professional learning seems to have been effective in particular contexts, or what kinds of professional learning in which schools and systems might most effectively invest. We should also consider what teachers and school leaders themselves consider to be their professional learning needs, especially as there can be a mismatch between scholarly understandings of PD and teacher understandings (Wong & Bautista, 2018).

Emily Lutrick and Susan Szabo (2012) found that school leaders think that professional learning should be ongoing, collaborative, and data- or interest-driven. In the US context, Darling-Hammond et al. (2009) found that teachers' top priorities for further professional development were:

- Learning more about the content they teach (23%);
- Classroom management (18%);
- Teaching students with special needs (15%); and
- Using technology in the classroom (14%).

These priorities are relevant to teachers' daily classroom practice and their work with students. They suggest that teachers want professional learning that helps them to be better teachers.

Carol Campbell et al. (2017) found that, in the Canadian context, teachers identified priority professional learning needs as:

- Knowledge, skills, and practices to support diverse learners' needs;
- Knowledge and understanding of Aboriginal people; and
- Subject and pedagogical knowledge, although the level of need varied by individual, career stage, school panel, school systems, and policy changes such as new curriculum and integration of technology expectations.

A survey of 507 teachers from the Republic of Ireland (Murphy & de Paor, 2017) revealed that teachers want professional learning that closely relates to their work in the classroom. These self-identified needs included:

- Curriculum and subject knowledge;
- Teaching, learning and assessment;
- Leadership and managing school change;
- Technology in the classroom; and
- Differentiation and addressing special educational needs.

The recent review of teacher registration in Australia found that discipline-specific learning should be an integral part of a teacher's overall professional learning (AITSL, 2018). One sub-recommendation was that Australian teacher registration should "explicitly specify that maintenance of proficiency against the Australian Professional Standards for Teachers includes up to date discipline-specific knowledge and skills relevant to their deployment and the curriculum they are expected to teach" (p.viii). This is related to the second Australia Professional Standard for Teachers: "Know the content and how to teach it" (AITSL, 2011), and clearly reflected in the above self-identified needs of teachers around subject, pedagogical, and technological knowledge.

The interdependent relationship between school and individual (Costa & Garmston, 2015) is crucial in professional learning. Teachers at different career stages have different professional learning needs. Newly graduated teachers benefit from mentoring, common team planning, a reduced course load and professional learning targeted to new teachers; while veteran teachers need their concerns listened to and addressed (DuFour et al., 2017). As professional capital is about individual and collective knowing and doing over time (Hargreaves & Fullan, 2012), professional learning works best when it addresses and honours parts and whole, person and group.

A word of warning

A central premise of this book is that professional learning, done well, can have a transformational influence on individuals, teams, schools, and systems, in ways that improve the relational aspects of schooling, organisational and system culture, and student achievement. It is important to note, however, that there is debate about the effectiveness of professional learning as a vehicle for positive change.

Some have suggested (e.g. Guskey & Yoon, 2009; Jacob & McGovern, 2015; Yoon et al., 2007) that we do not yet know what helps teachers to improve the quality of their instruction. It is certainly not as straightforward as professional learning hours equalling student learning improvement. Thomas Guskey and Kwang Suk Yoon (2009) state that "we have no strong, valid, and scientifically defensible evidence that these kinds of oft-promoted school-based professional learning are effective" (pp. 496–497). Their research synthesis found that, at that time, only nine of 1343 studies on teacher professional learning met the standards of credible evidence set by What Works Clearinghouse, the USA government body responsible for the provision of scientific evidence around education (Guskey & Yoon, 2009; Yoon et al., 2007). While the nine studies they analysed showed that providing professional development to teachers increased student achievement by an average of 21 percentile points, they describe the existing knowledge, about the relationship between professional learning activities and improvements in student learning, as scarce.

The value of professional learning efforts was questioned by the TNTP report (Jacob & McGovern, 2015) of a two-year study into teacher professional learning of over 10,000 teachers and 500 school leaders in three USA public school districts. They found that, despite schools and systems investing time and money into professional learning of teachers, no clear patterns emerged to suggest which deliberate efforts improved teacher performance. The authors arrive at the conclusion that those teachers who improve, according to district evaluation scores, have similar levels of satisfaction and similar mindsets to those who do not improve over time. The TNTP report suggests that we do not yet know what helps teachers to improve the quality of their instruction. Like Guskey and Yoon, they call for more rigorous evaluation of current professional development efforts.

Professional learning in the field of education is additionally susceptible to fads and solutions peddled by well-oiled corporate machines. As Helen Timperley (2008) points out, just because a method of professional development is popular, does not mean it is effective in impacting teachers' teaching and student outcomes. Unproven ideas, she argues, sweep through educational jurisdictions. There are also education concepts that, while often defined in research literature, take on a life of their own once they reach schools and become diluted or misused over time. When we are talking about modes of professional learning, it is important that we have a shared language, a common understanding of those terms we are using, preferably at system level, but at least at school level.

Schools are "nonlinear dynamical systems in which cause and effect are not tightly linked" and in which change happens in ways that researchers don't or can't suppose (Garmston & Wellman, 2013, p. 8). The multiple intersecting factors operating in schools make it difficult, if not impossible, to correlate a professional learning experience or intervention with changes in practice, culture, or student achievement. So while there is an increasing body of literature on the professional learning of educators, and trends have certainly emerged from research, the data on which these literatures are based needs close scrutiny, as do the consequent conclusions and recommendations. There remains a need for investigation of what it is that incites growth, change, and improvement in educators' practice, as well as impact on student achievement.

Despite these cautions, professional learning is at the heart of enriching our school systems, improving the learning and school experience of our students, and building the capacity of the teaching profession in ways that shift practice, encourage agency, and bring joy to the being and becoming of teaching and school leadership.

Spotlight on research: when and how professionals learn

As evident in the above discussion, there are plenty of studies on teacher professional learning. Many of these ask participants—via survey or interview—what professional learning opportunities have been offered to them and taken up by them. These kinds of studies consequently lead to findings around what the type of PD teachers have attended, or what course they enjoyed most or found most useful. These studies can tell us what teachers are attending that counts as PD in their schools and systems, but they do not interrogate whether learning has actually taken place.

My PhD study (Netolicky, 2016a) took a different, broader, approach, and resulted in broader findings. In interviews, I asked participants to "tell me about your experience of professional learning" and to explain "when you have professionally learned." In response, they cast their nets wider than their experiences in education sector work or related courses. Participants chose to discuss trans-formational vignettes, life experiences, and moments of realisation that would not necessarily be found on a survey on professional development. These self-reported professional learning examples included experiences that were:

- Professional and personal;
- Formal and informal;
- In and out of educational contexts; and
- Singular and collaborative (Netolicky, 2016a, 2016b).

The range of professional learning experiences found in this study are summar-ised in Table 1.1.

As the table indicates, and as pointed out by Andy Jacob & Kate McGovern (2015), teacher learning is highly individualised. There are a wide variety of experiences that teachers and school leaders consider to be times in which they have learned in ways that have shaped them professionally, including but also beyond school-based activities or courses labelled 'professional development.' This range of experiences are explored in more detail in the spotlights on research and practice in subsequent chapters. Professional learning interacts with professional identity and with non-professional life. Experiences that engage emotion and identity can have a transformational impact on teacher being and doing.

Spotlight on practice: teacher collaboration and lesson observation

An example of personally transformational learning for me is observing the les-sons of others and collaborating in teaching teams. Teaching is an intensely per-sonal act and teachers are very individualistic in their approaches. While this vulnerability and idiosyncrasy makes many teachers protective of their classroom, I have found being in other classrooms a powerful learning experience. Experi-encing how others do things differently reminds me of different ways of teach-ing, and reminds me about areas in which I might improve or experiment. Observations of others' teaching, in team teaching situations as a colleague, in my role as head of faculty, as a member of a peer coaching team, and as a senior leader, have had a direct impact on my own classroom practice. I have often found that seeing another teacher's lesson had a direct knock-on effect on my own subsequent lessons.

One particular class I remember observing was that of a literature class of a teacher I particularly admire. As head of faculty, I wandered in part way through and saw a buzz of excitement amid expert higher order questioning to provoke interesting cross-disciplinary thinking; lively discussion; students furiously writing notes as they heard each other's ideas and made new con-nections; the teacher seamlessly integrating technologies as enhancers of learn-ing; students crowding around the whiteboard-paint wall at the back of the classroom chatting and scribbling together in a collective outpouring of ana-lysis and exploration. After students were dismissed, they stayed on, not want-ing to leave the moment in which they were engrossed. The excitement and

Table 1.1 Tabulated summary of PhD findings about professional learning

Experience	Researcher	Teachers	Leaders	Professional	Personal	Formal	Informal	School context	Non-school contexts	Singular	Collaborative
Watching or working with educational role models and anti-models			✓	✓			✓	✓			✓
Collaborative work in schools	✓			✓		✓		✓			✓
Watching inspiring experts		✓		✓		✓	✓	✓	✓	✓	✓
Observing other teachers teach	✓		✓	✓		✓	✓	✓			✓
Relationships with coaches, mentors, and professional friends	✓		✓	✓		✓	✓	✓			✓
Connecting with others: conferences, associations, study, and online communities		✓	✓	✓		✓	✓	✓			✓
Reflecting, by self and with others			✓	✓		✓	✓	✓		✓	✓
Postgraduate study	✓		✓	✓	✓	✓	✓		✓	✓	✓
Pursuing own professional interests: professional reading and online platforms	✓		✓	✓	✓	✓	✓		✓	✓	✓
Non-educational workforce experience			✓	✓	✓	✓	✓		✓	✓	✓
Times and relationships with family	✓		✓	✓	✓		✓		✓	✓	✓
Travel			✓	✓	✓		✓	✓	✓	✓	✓
Tragedy			✓	✓	✓		✓	✓	✓	✓	✓
Quiet time and space to think			✓		✓		✓		✓	✓	✓

enthusiasm of the students resulted in my staying in this classroom to continue to experience their learning, rather than popping in and out as I had intended. Seeing such teacher and student excitement in a lesson reminded me of how engagement and technology can be married with rigour and scaffolding.

I can call to mind, too, the lessons I have observed in mathematics, science, and woodwork classrooms in which teachers have orchestrated the lesson through clear instruction, physical use of the classroom, and subtle non-verbal cues to manage student behaviour. I have learned much from being in early years classrooms with their use of learning stations, explicit instruction combined with play, and the physical environment as the 'third teacher.' Talking to the children in lessons can reveal to observer and teacher the depth of students' understanding and learning. Visiting the classrooms of colleagues makes me think that we should all visit each other's classrooms more often to experience the simultaneously deliberate and intuitive craft of teaching. Excellent teaching happens in classrooms daily and often goes unacknowledged or unshared.

Working in teams, both within a school and with teachers from other schools, is valuable learning for me. Calibrating expectations of student work through dialogue with other teachers, and planning learning programs together with other teachers, encourages me to make incremental changes to my practice. Watching other people teach, or teaching with others, are rewarding types of professional learning because they immediately provide examples in practice and a connection for conversation about teaching beliefs and craft. For two years I team taught with a teacher new to the school at which I was then working; we did not have an existing relationship and soon discovered that we had very different styles, approaches, values, and strengths. Our first instinct was to find a way to teach separately, but as our mandate was to literally teach our classes together, we were forced into a team relationship. As time went on, we found that our different ideas and strengths made us a great team, with our curriculum planning, pastoral care of students, and pedagogy all benefiting; we were better together. Differentiating for the needs of our students was made easier through flexible and deliberate grouping across the classes. While our collaborative relationship had initial teething problems, this co-teacher became a trusted friend and respected colleague. This was an early example of my growth emerging from a collaborative journey of discomfort, with benefits for me, my teaching partner, and the students.

These collaborative examples of self-identified transformation act as a window into the kinds of formal and informal collaborations and job-embedded experiences that can affect teachers' teaching.

Key takeaways

* Transformational professional learning is professional learning that shifts beliefs, and thereby behaviours of professionals. It is tied to an individual's personal and professional identity.
* Identity is the ongoing sense-making process of contextually-embedded perceived-selves-in-flux. It is an important consideration in professional learning for teachers and school leaders. It entails looking at who people are rather than how they perform.

- Research has found that effective professional learning is evidence-informed, job-embedded, aligned with school and system context, ongoing or sustained, and involves structured collaboration and elements of individual choice.
- Teachers want professional learning that makes them better teachers, including on subject knowledge, pedagogy, and behaviour management.
- Professional learning is a broad field with plenty of literature, but there remains a debate about its effectiveness and a need for investigation of what it is that incites growth, change, and improvement in educators' practice, as well as impact on student achievement.
- Observing other teachers teach, and teaching with other teachers, can be transformational for a teacher's practice, leading to changes in how they approach their own courses and classes.
- Teachers and school leaders professionally learn in ways that are professional and personal, formal and informal, in and out of educational contexts, and singular and collaborative.

References

Australian Institute for Teaching and School Leadership (AITSL). (2011). *Australian professional standards for teachers*. Carlton South: Education Council.

Australian Institute for Teaching and School Leadership (AITSL). (2012). *Australian charter for the professional learning of teachers and school leaders*. Carlton South: Education Council.

Australian Institute for Teaching and School Leadership (AITSL). (2018). *One teaching profession: Teacher registration in Australia*. Carlton South: Education Council.

Borg, S. (2011). The impact of in-service teacher education on language teachers' beliefs. *System, 39*(3), 370–380.

Bridges, D., Macklin, R., & Trede, F. (2012). Professional identity development: A review of the higher education literature. *Studies in Higher Education, 37*(3), 365–20.

Campbell, C., Osmond-Johnson, P., Faubert, B., Zeichner, K., & Hobbs-Johnson, A. (2017). *The state of educators' professional learning in Canada: Final research report*. Oxford: Learning Forward.

Costa, A. L., & Garmston, R. J. (2015). *Cognitive coaching: Developing self-directed leaders and learners*. London: Rowman & Littlefield.

Darling-Hammond, L., Wei, R. C., Andree, A., Richardson, N., & Orphanos, S. (2009). *Professional learning in the learning profession: A status report on teacher development in the U.S. and abroad*. Technical Report. Stanford: National Staff Development Council.

Darling-Hammond, L., & Steinhauser, C. (2012). *Greatness by Design: Supporting outstanding teaching to sustain a golden state*. Sacramento: California Department of Education.

Desimone, L. M. (2009). Improving impact studies of teachers' professional development: Toward better conceptualisations and measures. *Educational Researcher, 38*(3), 181–199.

Drago-Severson, E. (2009). *Leading adult learning: Supporting adult development in our schools*. Thousand Oaks: Corwin.

Drago-Severson, E., & Blum-DeStefano, J. (2018). *Leading change together: Developing educator capacity within schools and systems*. Alexandria: ASCD.

DuFour, R., DuFour, R., Eaker, R., Many, T. W., & Mattos, M. (2017). *Learning by doing: A handbook for professional learning communities at work* (3rd ed.). Moorabin: Hawker Brownlow Education.

Elliott, J. C. (2017). The evolution from traditional to online professional development: A review. *Journal of Digital Learning in Teacher Education, 33*(3), 114–125.

Fleming, J., & Kleinhenz, E. (2007). *Towards a moving school: Developing a professional learning and performance culture* Vol. 1. Camberwel: Australian Council for Educational Research.

Garmston, R. J., & Wellman, B. (2013). *Adaptive schools: A sourcebook for developing collaborative groups* (2nd ed.). Lanham: Rowman & Littlefield.

Glover, D., & Law, S. (1996). *Managing professional development in education: Issues in policy and practice*. London: Kogan Page.

Gonski, D., Arcus, T., Boston, K., Gould, V., Johnson, W., & O'Brien, L. (2018). *Through growth to achievement: The report of the review to achieve educational excellence in Australian schools*. Canberra: Commonwealth of Australia.

Gronn, P. (2003). *The new work of educational leaders: Changing leadership practice in an era of school reform*. London: Paul Chapman Publishing.

Guskey, T. R., & Yoon, K. S. (2009). What works in professional development? *The Phi Delta Kappan, 90*(7), 495–500.

Hargreaves, A., & Fullan, M. (2012). *Professional capital: Transforming teaching in every school*. Moorabbin: Hawker Brownlow Education.

Hargreaves, A., & O'Connor, M. T. (2018). *Collaborative professionalism: When teaching together means learning for all*. Thousand Oaks: Corwin.

Holland, D., Lachicotte, W., Skinner, D., & Cain, C. (1998). *Identity and agency in cultural worlds*. Cambridge: Harvard University.

Illeris, K. (2014). *Transformative learning and identity*. Abingdon: Routledge.

Jacob, A., & McGovern, K. (2015). *The mirage: Confronting the hard truth about our quest for teacher development*. New York: TNTP.

Lasky, S. (2005). A sociocultural approach to understanding teacher identity, agency, and professional vulnerability in a context of secondary school reform. *Teaching and Teacher Education, 21*, 899–916.

Lawler, S. (2014). *Identity: Sociological perspectives* (2nd ed.). Cambridge: Polity.

Learning Forward. (2011). *Standards for professional learning*. Oxford, OH: Learning Forward.

Lieberman, A., Campbell, C., & Yashkina, A. (2017). *Teacher leadership and learning: Of, by, and for teachers*. Abingdon: Routledge.

Lutrick, E., & Szabo, S. (2012). Instructional leaders' beliefs about effective professional development. *Delta Kappa Gamma Bulletin, 78*(3), 6–12.

Mockler, N. (2011). Becoming and 'being' a teacher: Understanding teacher professional identity. In N. Mockler & J. Sachs (Eds.). *Rethinking educational practice through reflexive inquiry* (pp. 123–138). Dordrecht: Springer.

Mockler, N. (2013). Teacher professional learning in a neoliberal age: Audit, professionalism and identity. *Australian Journal of Teacher Education, 38*(10), 35–47.

Muijs, D., Kyriakides, L., Van der Werf, G., Creemers, B., Timperley, H., & Earl, L. (2014). State of the art–teacher effectiveness and professional learning. *School Effectiveness and School Improvement, 25*(2), 231–256.

Murphy, T. R. N., & de Paor, C. (2017). Teachers' CPD and sectoral interests: Opportunities for convergence and divergence. *Teaching and Teacher Education, 66*, 242–249.

Netolicky, D. M. (2016a). *Down the rabbit hole: Professional identities, professional learning, and change in one Australian school* (Doctoral dissertation, Murdoch University).

Netolicky, D. M. (2016b). Rethinking professional learning for teachers and school leaders. *Journal of Professional Capital and Community, 1*(4), 270–285.

Netolicky, D. M. (2019). Elevating the professional identities and voices of teachers and school leaders in educational research, practice, and policymaking. In D. M. Netolicky, J. Andrews, & C. Paterson (Eds.). *Flip the system Australia: What matters in education* (pp. 9–18). Abingdon: Routledge.

Priestley, M., Biesta, G., & Robinson, S. (2015). *Teacher agency: An ecological approach*. London: Bloomsbury.

Rosenholtz, S. (1991). *Teachers' workplace: The social organisation of schools*. New York: Teachers College.

Shuler, M. K., Keller-Dupree, E., & Cook, K. (Eds.). (2017). *Transformational learning experiences: A conversation with counsellors and their personal and professional development journeys*. Lanham: Hamilton Books.

Thomas, M. A. M., & Mockler, N. (2018). Alternative routes to teacher professional identity: Exploring the conflated sub-identities of teach for America corps members. *Education Policy Analysis Archives*, *26*(6), 1–21.

Timperley, H. (2008). *Teacher professional learning and development: Educational practices series 18*. Brussels: International Academy of Education, International Bureau of Education & UNESCO.

Timperley, H., Wilson, A., Barrar, H., & Fung, I. (2007). *Teacher professional learning and development: Best evidence synthesis iteration*. Wellington: New Zealand Ministry for Education.

Wiliam, D. (2016). *Leadership for teacher learning: Creating a culture where all teachers improve so that all students succeed*. Moorabbin: Hawker Brownlow Education.

Wong, J., & Bautista, A. (2018). How do teachers define the notion of professional development? The case of primary music teachers. *Professional Development in Education*, *44*(4), 539–556.

Yoon, K. S., Duncan, T., Lee, S. W.-Y., Scarloss, B., & Shapley, K. (2007). *Reviewing the evidence on how teacher professional development affects student achievement (Issues & Answers Report, REL 2007–No. 033)*. Washington, DC: U.S. Department of Education, Institute of Education Sciences, National Centre for Education Evaluation and Regional Assistance, Regional Educational Laboratory Southwest.

Zepeda, S. J. (2013). *Professional development: What works* (2nd ed.). New York: Routledge.

Chapter 2

Speakers, courses, and conferences

Often when those working in schools think about professional learning they think about those opportunities advertised as such. That is courses, conferences, lectures, workshops, and keynotes by a variety of speakers offered up to teachers and school leaders as experiences intended to facilitate learning and improvement. These are the kinds of promoted events that come across the desks, into the email inboxes, and into the pigeonholes, of teachers and school leaders around the world. Companies are built around providing professional learning to those working in schools, and the subjects of these offerings are diverse. They cover leadership, teaching, student wellbeing, pastoral care, particular subjects, different teaching methodologies, data use, and technologies for learning. They are run by organisations and consultants. They are rarely run by practising teachers and school leaders, although many conferences offer concurrent sessions in which practising educators share their practice (usually for free, while consultants are paid for their time, preparation, and expertise).

This kind of professional learning is widespread. Linda Darling-Hammond et al. (2009) found that more than nine out of ten teachers in the USA have participated in professional learning consisting primarily of short term conferences or workshops. Fewer teachers participated in other forms of traditional professional learning, including university courses related to teaching (36%) and observational visits to other schools (22%). While direct instruction as a mode of adult learning can be meaningful and effective, the constructivist theory of learning—that learners construct their own knowledge, especially in the context of adult learning—has influenced thinking around professional learning modes (Elliott, 2017), leading to more attempts at interactive course design, and more sustained relationships between schools and consultants, universities, or companies, rather than a present-and-run approach.

While traditional workshops and speakers are often criticised as the 'poster child' of ineffective professional learning practice (Yoon et al., 2007), they can and do provide effective professional learning. Traditional professional learning activities provide teachers and school leaders with a broader context than their own school (Burstow, 2018). We chat over coffee with local or national colleagues who have similar professional interests, and find out what's happening in other schools, as well as hearing from experts who can bring a useful lens to the work of teachers and school leaders. External expertise is necessary in educators' professional learning (Timperley, 2008). We cannot exist in a vacuum in our schools, and our work benefits from outside knowledge and perspectives.

I currently oversee the budget, operation, and agenda of professional learning in my school, a role that I describe in more detail in Chapter 8. This means, in part, being the gatekeeper of professional learning spending. We have processes for staff to apply for professional learning, and decision making frameworks to help line managers and I decide if the professional learning is appropriate and within budget. On application, staff have to articulate how the professional learning aligns with their own professional goals, the school and team goals; and how it will be of benefit to themselves, their team, or their students. Sometimes groups of staff attend a single professional learning experience together, in order to facilitate continued discussions and implementation on their return to school. At other times highly motivated individuals attend a course and bring back that learning to their teams and to their own practice. In addition to teachers and school leaders attending conferences and courses, we employ external experts internally, to speak to or work with our staff. The challenge for educators is finding the time and head space to bring external professional learning to life, back at school when the busyness of the job kicks back in.

Spotlight on research: course and conference learning

My PhD participants articulated that they professionally learned from traditional professional learning, although much traditional professional learning was seen as an act of compliance, rather than an experience of learning. Their responses support Yoon et al.'s (2007) findings that workshops, often criticised for being isolated and ineffective methods of developing teachers, should not be wholly dismissed as ineffective practice, but can provide effective professional learning. While often thought of as transactional learning, a number of participants discussed speakers or courses that had made a difference to their beliefs and practices. One teacher described an inspiring speaker who had completely changed their thinking. The experience of hearing this speaker was something that stayed with them in their lessons when they were making pedagogical decisions and responding to their students. A soundbite from a presenter was held onto by some participants for years into their practice, as an anchor or key message to which they returned.

Teacher participants were critical of professional learning that uses ineffective teaching methods or commodifies educational theory and practice. They were cynical of the sales pitch of professional learning providers and of the tendency for professional learning to offer apparently new ways to think about or 'do' education. They were frustrated by professional learning that "just tells you the same kinds of things but calls it something different" or is couched in "glitzy packaging."

The effectiveness of professional learning courses was a point of divergence of leader participants. Three middle leaders said that they could always get something out of a course, while two executive leaders and one middle leader explained that for them courses were mostly not worth their time. For executive leaders this was partly due to the impacts of being taken out of the school environment and role, and partly because they perceived that traditional professional learning activities do not change practice or transform thought. One explained that "going externally or having external people come in to tell me things … won't change my practice eight times out of 10."

Returning to being learners themselves facilitated my PhD participants' reflections on their own learning, and their leading of the learning of others. Being in a classroom or course, and participating in further study, was a reminder of what it is like to be a student and that "one size does not fit all" in terms of professional learning. There's nothing like having to sit through a bad course—in which the content is pitched badly and the pedagogy is ineffective—to remind a teacher what it's like to be a student in an unproductive classroom. In this way professional learning experiences had the unexpected effect of helping teachers reflect on their own practice through the eyes of their students. They asked themselves: What is it like to be in my lesson? What is the experience for my students? How might I channel or avoid what I am currently experiencing in this session, in my own classroom?

Six leader participants had completed their Masters study and all considered it a significant professional learning experience. For one middle leader, their Masters was a challenging course with content they found "impenetrable." Their struggle to grasp the course material allowed them to "understand how some students feel" when they grapple with content or skills. This epiphanic experience is one that the leader always keeps in their mind because "that's how some kids feel with learning." One leader talked about their Masters study as "the most significant piece of learning" they had done. It had become a part of who they are. Another discussed the importance of theory informing practice; the professional reading and collaboration of their Masters course reinvigorated their work back at school.

A comment that I made in one of the researcher interviews for my PhD mirrors one I hear often from colleagues. While being interviewed by the external interviewer, I mused that those professional learning experiences I find useful are carefully crafted around the learner and take on board effective teaching practices. Often they involve doing or talking, rather than just listening. I said:

> I seek out formal professional learning opportunities, but if I think about the things that are called 'professional learning' or 'PD,' I haven't necessarily professionally learned, just because it's called 'professional development.' Often it is the conversations with colleagues that happen afterwards which are most important.

Connections and discussions with colleagues from within a school, or with others from other networks or schools, is often seem the most useful part of a traditional professional learning experience. After attending a weekend-long conference with nine colleagues, for example, the group of us formed a professional learning group in order to work through, implement, and immerse ourselves in the thinking to which we had been exposed. We met for lunches and organised termly evening get-togethers to discuss our career ideas, explore work/life challenges, and share professional reading.

My PhD participants' responses revealed that traditional forms of professional learning have their uses, and can lead to learning, although this might not be what is planned for or expected by organisers of those courses. It was sometimes the content of a keynote or workshop that sparked thinking, and sometimes it was the delivery of a professional learning session that was a reminder of what not to do in the classroom. Conferences and courses provided these teachers and school leaders with the space to reflect, have professional conversations, and make connections with other professionals. The in-between conference spaces were where much conference learning happened.

Spotlight on practice: conference attendance

Like all teachers, my professional learning has included in-house school-based professional learning, as well as conferences, as both participant and presenter, in areas of interest to me such as my subject area, technologies, leadership, and education research. I have been lucky to work at schools that have had the resources to send me to a variety of professional learning opportunities, although I have also self-funded my attendance at some conferences. Being given the opportunity to self-choose conferences of interest and attend these has given me a sense of ownership over the trajectory of my learning. Listening to renowned keynote speakers, educators sharing their practice, or leaders sharing their stories, is professionally invigorating. Yet I have often found myself captivated in the moment by a charismatic and entertaining speaker, but walking out of the room wondering what on earth all that energy and comedy has to do with my actual practice. It often hasn't changed anything about what I believe or what I do as a professional. I may have generated recordable professional learning hours by attending a keynote, but there hasn't been learning, let alone transformational learning.

Examples of influential courses for my own learning that come to mind include the adaptive schools course, the cognitive coaching course, and GROWTH coaching training. These have provided theory, examples of the theory in practice, and opportunities for rich discussion with colleagues. I've also attended traditional education and education leadership conferences that usually provide some interesting or energising sessions, and an excellent opportunity to have professional conversations with educators from other schools.

The example that follows is perhaps an unusual one, that may not resonate with the experiences of other teachers and school leaders. I explore it here partly because it demonstrates the kinds of learning that conferences can provide. I also use it as a seed for the thought that sometimes a challenging or left-of-centre conference, outside of our usual networks and echo chambers, can be an experience that incites meaningful professional learning and takes us beyond our usual ways of thinking.

Despite being a conference not often thought of as one for teachers and leaders in schools (unless they are undertaking a research degree), the Australian Association for Research in Education (AARE) national conference has made a difference to my teaching and school leadership practice. At the time of writing I have attended this conference four years running, from 2015 to 2018, including three years in which I presented one or more papers. I am an atypical attendee of this conference; delegates are mostly made up of educators working in universities. Perhaps it is the discomforting feeling of being on the periphery of the delegation that has meant that the AARE conference has provoked my professional thinking.

Attending others' presentations

I have attended AARE sessions from multiple thematic areas, rather than committing to one common thread throughout the conference. I tend to spread my time between sessions relevant to my own research and practice, and those that interest me outside of my normal bubble. Sometimes it is attending a session from well outside of my own area that sparks in me the kernel of a way to think about something differently. Those presentations within my area help me to better understand the field and consider the place of my own work in the context of others. As a boundary-spanning pracademic, currently responsible for research and evidence use in my school, the conference keeps me up to date with current education research.

At this conference I have been exposed to rigorous scholarship, but also to researchers grappling with the complexities of their work. This public wrestling with education knowledge shows me that research and knowledge are constantly evolving, and that it is ok to have thinking that is a work in progress. In some of the sessions I have attended, very experienced academics have presented as-yet-unformed ideas. They have shared and modelled the ways in which they explore a theorist they are reading for the first time, or work through a newborn idea. The vulnerability of these academics—willing to present the workings-out of their practice and not just the result of layered years of thinking—has been an example for me in being publicly vulnerable, embracing what I don't know, and working through discomfort to interrogate gaps in my own knowledge. It also reminds me as a school practitioner about the limits and fallibilities of research; it can tell us some things, but we need to interrogate it carefully and consider how it relates to our context.

Like attending any conference, a visit to AARE provides a break from the busy daily routine of teaching and leading. While the program is busy, it allows delegates to listen to, cogitate on, and talk about those arenas of education in which they wish to immerse themselves. During the conference I give myself permission to stop and be engrossed in research related to my work, to make time and space for thinking, and to engage in robust conversation. I live and breathe teaching and leading for most of the year, but here for a few days I get to engage with different ways of considering and improving that daily work. It gives me time to contemplate: What does current educational research have to say about education practice? How might I—as teacher, school leader, and researcher—positively influence my own contexts, as well as broader narratives of education?

Presenting at a conference

I find that presenting at conferences is an opportunity to communicate and publicly explore my work and thinking. Presenting helps me to refine the precision of my ideas and effectiveness of my communication by asking questions of myself. How have I titled my presentation? How have I designed my slides? How have I distilled the essence of my paper down to a 20-minute presentation? The decision making required in order to present to an audience helps to refine ideas, clarify theory, and fine-tune language. It also allows me to contribute to the education space, sharing ideas and practice with others.

Presenting also means inviting others to engage with my work. Discussion after a presentation can provide the opportunity for the presenter to clarify and extend their thinking, thanks to questions, comments, and provocations from the audience. In this way, conference presentations can help to refine ideas and develop thinking of both audience and presenter.

Connecting with others at a conference

Like any conference that I attend more than once, at AARE I have begun to see patterns of those who attend these conferences and those who are active in that professional community. As I am active on Twitter, there have been many additional familiar faces in the room. That's one thing I enjoy about professional social media: that it allows me to walk into a room in which I've barely met anyone, yet feel like I know a number of people. Recognising scholars attending the conference spills over into conversations over breakfast, coffee, lunch, and dinner. So the conference program (as is so often the case) is only one layer of learning, thinking, and conversing; much of the discussion happens in the in-between conference spaces. At the AARE conference, delegates (including early career researchers school-leader-scholar-boundary-spanners like myself, and professors) have engaged me, questioned me, encouraged me, and directly challenged me. This is about being in a community unafraid to be critical with one another. These liminal conference spaces can offer rewarding learning experiences.

The AARE conference is a personal example of an opportunity to connect with educators across a wide range of Australian and international organisations, who approach education in a variety of ways, through multiple different lenses. Many experienced or well-known academics are very open to meeting early career researchers, doctoral candidates, and school practitioners, and most are generous with their time and their advice. This conference connects me with Australian scholarship, often lacking in Australian professional education conferences, which so often fly in international experts to share their views on how we might do education better.

Key takeaways

- Traditional professional learning, such as speakers, courses, and conferences, should not be written off as ineffective learning. They have their place and can provide effective professional learning.
- Attending conferences and traditional professional learning opportunities can provide content learning that shapes teachers' and school leaders' thinking.
- Traditional professional learning like conferences and courses often provides space for thinking, networking, and professional conversation and connection. It is often between sessions or during break time, with colleagues from their own or other schools, that teachers and school leaders develop their thinking.
- Teachers and school leaders need the time and head space to bring external professional learning to life, back at school when the busyness of the job kicks back in.

References

Burstow, B. (2018). *Effective teacher development: Theory and practice in professional learning*. London: Bloomsbury.

Darling-Hammond, L., Wei, R. C., Andree, A., Richardson, N., & Orphanos, S. (2009). *Professional learning in the learning profession: A status report on teacher development in the U.S. and abroad*. Technical Report. Stanford: National Staff Development Council.

Elliott, J. C. (2017). The evolution from traditional to online professional development: A review. *Journal of Digital Learning in Teacher Education, 33*(3), 114–125.

Timperley, H. (2008). *Teacher professional learning and development: Educational practices series 18*. Brussels: International Academy of Education, International Bureau of Education & UNESCO.

Yoon, K. S., Duncan, T., Lee, S. W.-Y., Scarloss, B., & Shapley, K. (2007). *Reviewing the evidence on how teacher professional development affects student achievement (Issues & Answers Report, REL 2007–No. 033)*. Washington, DC: U.S. Department of Education, Institute of Education Sciences, National Centre for Education Evaluation and Regional Assistance, Regional Educational Laboratory Southwest.

Chapter 3

Key life moments as professional learning

Professional learning is often listed as a series of things educators can do, like those experiences discussed above for which teachers and school leaders register, and that they attend at a particular time and place: courses, activities, seminars, workshops. This chapter argues that professional learning that shapes beliefs and practices occurs across life, school, and work (Netolicky, 2016a).

Implicit and informal professional learning is largely invisible, neglected, and under-researched (Evans, 2019). There is a reluctance for organisations to recognise informal learning and its significance (Eraut, 2012). Michael Eraut (2012) identifies three types of early career learning:

- *Work processes with learning as a by-product.* E.g. working alongside others, problem solving, participating in group processes.
- *Learning activities located within work or learning processes.* E.g. listening and observing, giving and receiving feedback, locating resource people.
- *Learning processes at or near the workplace.* E.g. shadowing, visiting other sites, independent study.

It is not just job-embedded experiences that shape the beliefs and practices of educators. Personal experience, too, shapes teacher professional beliefs and practices. Mark Priestley et al. (2015) argue that professional experience is perhaps less significant than personal experience in shaping teacher agency.

As I explain in Chapter 1, professional learning was shown by my PhD study to be professional *and* personal, formal *and* informal, in *and* out of educational contexts, and singular *and* collaborative. When my PhD participants were asked to tell me about when, where, and how they had professionally learned—that is, what experiences had shaped them as teachers and leaders—their responses did not reflect the kind of PD hours-tallying approach of teacher registration bodies and professional associations. Rather, their answers, stories, and reflections revealed that professional learning deeply involves sense of self (Netolicky, 2016b). For example, teachers and leaders explained how their beliefs and practices shifted through experiences such as listening to an inspiring speaker, being managed by an ineffective leader, doing volunteer work, or travelling to third world countries and seeing the realities of life for others around the world. Postgraduate study was found to fulfil needs for self-learning and furthering career ambition. Teachers and school leaders talked about their individual goals and learning experiences, as well as those that were instrumental because of their collaborative nature. For teacher participants, collaboration with others encouraged open mindedness and changes in thinking, shaping their views about teaching practice and encouraging talking between teachers about how to get better and why they might want to get better. Leaders, too, discussed the balance between self and group, individual and organisation, in their own learning and in their leading of others' learning. These individuals learned from teachers and leaders who they considered to be the best, to be emulated, and the worst, to be avoided. Teachers and school leaders learn, and build their identities from, those professionals with whom they work, and even teachers they had at school.

As I discussed in Chapter 1, identity is a key consideration when reflecting on professional learning. My own fluid and blurred identity feeds into my thinking around professional learning. I have a teacher identity, a leader identity, a coach identity, a researcher identity, a writer identity, a family identity. While researchers, schools, and professional bodies fixate on formal and easily recognisable professional learning, educators cannot separate their personal lives from their work lives or their personal selves from their professional selves. Personal and professional identities are interwoven (Robertson, 2017), and our understanding of professional learning should reflect this.

Spotlight on research: wider life experiences

My PhD asked participants to describe their lived experiences of their contextually-embedded perceived-selves-in-flux, accepting Nicole Mockler's (2011) argument that the storied nature of identity lends itself to description, rather than definition. The school leaders in my PhD study saw themselves as teachers first and foremost, and leaders second; the student was at the centre of their senses of self. It is wider life experiences, as well as professional experiences, that shift professional beliefs and practices. The educators in my study viewed professional learning as something that happened, not just in work or work-related experiences, but throughout their lives. I said when being interviewed for my PhD study that "it is other things in school or in life or in relationships that have changed what I do professionally, rather than a course that says that it will." Personal examples that participants considered to be professional learning experiences included family experiences and relationships, travel, tragedy, and space for self.

Formative professional learning experiences included important relationships in educators' lives. All participants—teachers, leaders, and me as embedded researcher interviewee—discussed pivotal personal and professional relationships that were ongoing learning experiences. For example, one leader summarised the importance of life experiences in professional learning, identities, beliefs and behaviours, when they said, "My whole life has probably shaped who I've become." One leader talked about the "huge influence" of their grandmother; "a very strong woman and a very resilient woman. But always there, always on the periphery, always there if you needed her." I discussed the narratives of my parents as part of my own professional story.

For two participants, becoming and being a parent profoundly impacted professional identities and practices. Experiences of school teachers were also foundational in shaping teacher identities. One leader had "vivid memories of teachers who knew their stuff" and who "went way above and beyond the call to find whatever avenue they could get to get their kids to get their stuff," including one who held seminars at her home. This leader's "memorable teachers" were those who revealed themselves "as people," disclosing who they were within and beyond the classroom and showing an interest in students within and beyond the classroom. These personal relationships shape educators' self-perceptions, beliefs, and professional practices.

The participants in my PhD study discussed the influence of positive job-embedded relationships such as professional mentors, school leaders, professional coaches, and professional friends. Many talked about these as relationships that developed naturally, rather than ones that were imposed by the school. That is, they often weren't 'buddy' teachers, assigned mentors, or line managers. Leaders discussed the importance of those leaders who had identified something in them, and encouraged them or tapped them on the shoulder for a promotional opportunity. Two leaders saw themselves as the bower bird who picks and chooses aspects of leadership to adopt from their observation of other leaders. This metaphor allowed the leaders to explain their identities in terms of a bird that builds a nest from specially selected observed behaviours and characteristics of others' leadership, giving a sense of leadership as built over time, and affected by experiences, in this case of other leaders.

Anti-models also shaped the participants of this study; that is, those teachers or leaders they *didn't* want to emulate. One leader recounted an experience of a "negative" leader who "used to write down all the things I wasn't doing right and then hand them to me on a Friday ... she never gave me any positives, and I need praise." As a result of this continuous "overwhelming" and "basically negative" feedback, which was given without discussion, this leader "almost stopped" teaching, but now sees "a direct correlation" between that experience and the way they operate as a leader. It was formative in shaping the kind of leader they aspired to be: "telling people what they're doing well" rather than being too "fixated on the things that need improving." One teacher noted, "I don't want to become one of those old jaded teachers." Participants strove to be different to those who had made them feel small, or who they had perceived as being ineffective. While these are work-based experiences, their informality places them outside the realm of what would be considered professional learning. They reveal, however, that educators learn through real-life models of who they admire and to whom they aspire, as well as those who enrage, disappoint, and belittle.

For one teacher, one leader, and me (as I explain in the following spotlight on practice), travel emerged as a transformational experience that impacted on professional identity. For another teacher, volunteering in an out of school mentoring program with disadvantaged youth was a "leveller" that stopped them "from taking things for granted and makes me realise that this little bubble isn't reality." A leader had been shaped through working with teachers in a third world orphanage. It changed their perspective and helped them to realise the privileged position of those in their own country and school. "We take for granted what we see as hardships, which are actually to them privileges." This leader knew that "those kids and those teachers would give anything for the difficulties we face in life." So when school leadership becomes stressful, "I put myself back on the balcony in 45 degrees, no running water, no power, cold potato curry for dinner. It's actually alright." In this case, travel and service influenced professional identity, beliefs, and behaviour.

Becoming a parent was a catalytic professional identity shaping experience shared by two participants. For one, this life milestone meant a "shift in work/life balance" and the realisation that constantly working "doesn't necessarily make you a better teacher." Parenting allowed this teacher to understand and empathise with parents, and resist blaming parents for their children's behaviours.

My PhD data reveals that professional learning and growth can be surprising, nonlinear, and messy. For instance, the teachers and I, while observing lessons for the purposes of coaching others, found that observing the lessons of others impacted our own teaching practice; we found ourselves borrowing or drawing from other teachers' teaching. These kinds of unexpected learning happenings reflect Mark Smylie's (1995) discussion of unplanned, incidental learning that occurs in surprising and unpredictable ways. They also resonate with David Clarke and Hilary Hollingsworth's (2002) interconnected and nonlinear model of professional learning. Seemingly minor or unexpected moments can have substantial impacts on educators and their practices (Garmston & Wellman, 2013); they can be vital for the growth and transformation of teachers and leaders. Data from this study show that relationships, conversations, and life events have the potency to shift core beliefs, shape senses of self, and alter learning trajectories, in nonlinear, viral, and synaptic ways. Small things, not necessarily called 'professional learning' or 'professional development,' can be catalysts for deep and lasting personal learning and individual change.

Through the participant voices of my PhD, professional learning was shown to be a lifelong process made up of epiphanic life moments that are professional and personal, formal and informal, in schools and out of schools, singular and collaborative. Transformation of educators' identities and practices occur in environments that are supportive, challenging, and growth-focused, rather than evaluation-driven. My PhD drew together and built upon others who had explored the valuing of epiphanies or critical moments, and suggested that differentiation of professional learning opportunities would allow educators to choose individual or collaborative ways into their own growth. In looking to teachers and leaders themselves for their perceptions of when learning had been transformational, the stories of this study suggest that professional learning interacts with professional identity. It is that which taps into who educators see and feel they are that has the most impact on beliefs, thoughts, behaviours, and practices (Netolicky, 2016a, 2016b).

Spotlight on practice: travel as professional learning

Sometimes professional learning can look like travel. Literature-related visits to Shakespeare's Globe Theatre in London or Casa di Giulietta in Verona, or art-related visits to galleries, may be considered professional learning for teachers of these subjects. Languages teachers learn professionally by spending time in the countries of origin of the language they are teaching. Other travel is unlikely to be considered professional learning, but it still has a role in transforming those teachers and school leaders privileged enough to be able to travel.

Independent travel is something that shapes my identity as an educator. When I travel to unfamiliar places, I am in a state of heightened awareness, of noticing, of immersing myself in new languages, cultures, and people. I lie on footpaths and in fields to take pictures. I am fascinated by the seemingly wondrous minutiae of the world around me, such as haphazard roof-top aerials in Portugal, badly translated signs in China, and the manes of Icelandic horses. I recall spending one evening in the back of an Istanbul café smelling the owner's homemade sheesha tobacco and guessing the flavours, and another drumming in a circle of musicians in Marrakech's Jemaa el-Fna. Travelling independently in Russia required navigating inter-city train ticket buying, Metro travel, negotiating the Cyrillic alphabet, and hearing stories of police corruption. I remember vividly the night I called my husband from Denizli bus station in Turkey; it was 11pm and I was waiting for a mini bus, the only woman in sight and feeling uneasy. Another night, on another trip, I went searching through a dark forest for an abandoned fortress on a Croatian island, with two friends and a couple of Zagrebians we had met on the ferry. It was made all the more interesting when we were later told by locals that the forest still had landmines from when it was a naval base. Apparently the 34 mines left over from World War Two have since been cleared from the island.

These moments of engagement with people and places happen when immersed in the travelling mindset of receptivity and openness to learning. Travelling to a place where the language and culture are very different from my own, and I must work to understand and make myself understood, is an invigorating challenge that immerses me in intense learning. It reminds me of what real-life learning looks like and of the privileges and idiosyncrasies of my own country and the lives of my students. It contextualises the knowledge and skills I teach within a broader international frame.

Examples of work-based travel are two of the most powerful professional experiences of my career, and I explain them next: travelling to China for five weeks with a group of 60 students, and a one-week professional fellowship to New York to investigate the use of coaching in schools.

The world as classroom: five weeks in China with 60 students

Some years ago, a colleague and I were responsible for taking 60 Australian students to an international campus in China for five weeks. My colleague and I were the pastoral support component of the experience for students; as the teachers they knew from school in Australia, we provided knowledge of those students and emotional support for them. The educational program was run by a head of campus and teachers who spoke both English and Mandarin. The five week learning program itself was based on real world experience; students explored the sights, streets, shops, and eateries of the places we went, responsible for their own transport, map-reading, food-ordering, and bill-paying.

Professionally, this experience stayed with me for a number of reasons. It highlighted for me the essentialness of pastoral relationships with students. One of the students in my group had just discovered that they had Long QT syndrome, which required them to carry a defibrillator at all times, and for teachers to be trained in its use, should we need to restart the student's heart. Without the student's parents around, I often counselled the student in the middle of the night, talking through concerns and fears. The student's sense of awe and achievement at being atop the Great Wall was a reminder to me of the compelling experiences both education and travel can provide.

This experience of accompanying students on a travel and learning experience showed me the impact of real-life, authentic learning for students, particularly those for whom 'normal' school is difficult. Teachers in this context were problem-setters and facilitators. Each morning they set students a challenge for the day, such as to see a particular sight. Students then spent time planning how they would get there, where they would eat, how they would pay, and how they would keep track of each other. This experiential pedagogy allowed students to collaborate in constructing their own solutions. It opened up possibilities and questions for me about what a classroom might look like, and about what and how students might learn. These students were outside their comfort zones and needed support while being allowed to grow. They expressed a sense that the program allowed them to mature as it encouraged them to succeed and assumed their capacity to do things they found challenging.

Self-directed travelling professional fellowship: New York

In 2014 I was fortunate to receive a travelling fellowship in order to undertake an investigative series of visits to schools and universities in and around New York. This included teachers, school leaders, Ellie Drago-Severson at Columbia University's Teachers College, and Charlotte Danielson and Cindy Tocci in Princeton. The aim was to further my own learning and to bring back insights that would contribute to the strategic direction of the school and to the design and implementation of a coaching intervention intended to improve teaching. While I had help connecting with some people and organisations, I organised the visits, flights, transport, and accommodation. My learning schedule was my own. This was self-directed and organisation-supported professional learning travel which was driven by me as the learner and involved collaboration with others from outside of my normal professional sphere. It was experiential, real world, and deeply immersive.

Part of my learning experience was an experiment in social media. I had decided to use a blog to record my thinking. This was partly intended as an accountability measure to the school; it would record and share what I was doing and learning as I went. It was also a kind of public online journal that opened my thinking up to the interactions of other educators. My blog theeduflaneuse.com was born. I was able to share my work and thinking with not only those back at my own school, but with others from around the world: educators, thought leaders, researchers, students, people in other industries, friends, and like-minded individuals. After the trip, I shared my blog posts with those I had met while in New York. This sparked further conversations and kept the dialogue and learning going after the learning experience had officially come to a close. Blogging and tweeting helped me to be in a constant place of self-reflective and collaborative learning, and to extend this state to before and after the formal learning experience.

Key takeaways

Professional learning can happen in unexpected places and in unexpected ways.

- Life moments can act like epiphanies that change a person's beliefs and thereby change the way they see themselves as professionals, or the ways in which they approach or do their job.
- Job-embedded experiences, personal and work relationships, postgraduate study, teachers, role models, anti-models, parenting, and travel can all provide critical moments that shape teacher and leader identity, and thereby influence professional practice.
- It is that which taps into who educators see and feel they are that has the most impact on beliefs, thoughts, behaviours, and practices.

References

Clarke, D., & Hollingsworth, H. (2002). Elaborating a model of teacher professional growth. *Teaching and Teacher Education, 18*(8), 947–967.

Eraut, M. (2012). Developing a broader approach to professional learning. In A. Mc Kee & M. Eraut (Eds.). *Learning trajectories, Innovation and identity for professional development* (pp. 21–46). Dordrecht: Springer.

Evans, L. (2019). Implicit and informal professional development: What it 'looks like', how it occurs, and why we need to research it. *Professional Development in Education, 45*(1), 3–16.

Garmston, R. J., & Wellman, B. (2013). *Adaptive schools: A sourcebook for developing collaborative groups* (2nd ed.). Lanham: Rowman & Littlefield.

Mockler, N. (2011). Becoming and 'being' a teacher: Understanding teacher professional identity. In N. Mockler & J. Sachs (Eds.). *Rethinking educational practice through reflexive inquiry* (pp. 123–138). Dordrecht: Springer.

Netolicky, D. M. (2016a). *Down the rabbit hole: Professional identities, professional learning, and change in one Australian school* (Doctoral dissertation, Murdoch University).

Netolicky, D. M. (2016b). Rethinking professional learning for teachers and school leaders. *Journal of Professional Capital and Community, 1*(4), 270–285.

Priestley, M., Biesta, G., & Robinson, S. (2015). *Teacher agency: An ecological approach*. London: Bloomsbury.

Robertson, S. (2017). Transformation of professional identity in an experienced primary school principal: A New Zealand case study. *Educational Management Administration & Leadership, 45*(5), 774–789.

Smylie, M. A. (1995). Teacher learning in the workplace: Implications for school reform. In T. R. Guskey & M. Huberman (Eds.). *Professional development in education: New paradigms and practices* (pp. 92–113). New York: Teachers College.

Chapter 4

Collaborative professional learning

In 1990 Judith Warren Little noted the "present enthusiasm for teacher collaboration" (p. 509), and in 2017 Darling-Hammond called teacher collaboration "the next emerging horizon for teacher learning" (p. 304). In 2012 the *Australian Charter for the professional learning of teachers and school leaders* named collaboration as one of the characteristics of high quality professional learning. Collaboration is generally agreed to be one of the best ways to develop teaching, learning, and leading, and grow individual and organisational capacity (Drago-Severson & Blum-DeStefano, 2018). Andy Hargreaves and Michael O'Connor (2018) assert that "the evidence that, in general, professional collaboration benefits students and teachers alike has become almost irrefutable" (p. 3), but add that collaboration needs to be deliberately designed around effective practice. Teacher and school leader collaboration has been promoted for decades as a vehicle through which schools can develop the effectiveness of their core work: teaching and learning. This chapter outlines the importance of opportunities for collaboration and collective effort in professional learning.

Bob Garmston and Bruce Wellman (2013) give an elegant introduction to the notion of professionals learning and working together as a community:

> The word *professional* has its roots in *profess*, meaning to declare, to own, and to claim some body of knowledge; it therefore implies a level of expertise with a strong technical core that can be clearly articulated by practitioners. The word *community* has its roots in the word *common*, and its relationship to the word *communicate* implies that the body of expertise is shared. The practitioners in a professional community talk regularly about their collective practice and work together to extend and effectively apply this knowledge base (p. 13).

Collaborative professional learning is about the expertise of individual teachers being leveraged in a group so that students and teachers benefit. It can allow teachers to focus on their teaching. This sounds like an obvious statement to make, but much professional learning remains about peripheral teacher work, rather than focused on student learning, curriculum design, content knowledge, and classroom pedagogy.

Relationships and community

Teaching is a profession grounded in notions of care and service. Teachers are expected to give each other help, but at the same time they tend not to step in with unsolicited advice to colleagues (Little, 1990). The engine behind the momentum to increase collaborative professional learning in education is the belief that when teachers work together—when vision, purpose, and practice are shared—teachers and school leaders are energised, better informed, make better decisions, improve their knowledge and practice, and improve student learning and achievement.

However, a group of teachers in a meeting, or called a 'team,' does not collaboration or collaborative professional learning make. As Laura Lipton and Bruce Wellman (2013) note, "being in the room doesn't mean individuals necessarily identify as members of the group or think of themselves as interlocking parts of the whole" (p. 2). In collaborative professional learning, relationships are key. This is because professional learning is a *situated social practice* and *collective process* profoundly affected by environment (Hargreaves & Fullan, 2012; Wenger, 2000), and by the social networks in personal and professional contexts. The people involved in professional collaboration influence its effects and success. Positional power and the ecosystem of relationships need to be taken into consideration, otherwise collaboration can be guarded and manufactured, rather than open and productive.

The notion of a *holding environment* resonates. First introduced by Winnicott (1960) in psychoanalytic literature, it has been appropriated in educational contexts (Drago-Severson, 2012; Drago-Severson & Blum-DeStefano, 2018). In educational contexts, it is an organisational environment that meets learners where they are, and offers high support and high challenge in order to foster adult growth. Ellie Drago-Severson (2012) notes that in order for teachers to feel held by their professional environments, those environments require a "keen awareness for individual needs and differences, and a willingness to honour and see those in our care for who they are and who they are becoming" (p. 47). Collaborative professional groups need to exist in an environment that provides both high support and high challenge.

Feeling good does not mean learning is happening

Professional relationships on their own, or a feeling of enjoyment when working together with colleagues, should not be mistaken for professional learning. Enjoying a professional experience of collaboration does not equal effective professional learning, and professional learning is not an exercise in wellbeing.

All teachers have been to a conference workshop or team building exercise that we liked, or during which we had feel-good conversations with colleagues, but we walked away thinking: That was fun, but what was the point of it? For example, during one staff PD day at a school in which I was working, an international education consultant took the staff through a two-hour workshop on how to karate chop a wooden board in half. I remember feeling entertained and empowered when I successfully split my board in half with my bare hands, but I can't remember the point of the exercise. It was memorable, but has not had an impact on me as a teacher or leader.

As Jeffrey Carpenter and Jayme Linton (2016) point out, teacher enthusiasm for, or fun during, professional learning does not equate to meaningful or lasting impact for students. Collaboration that results in positive feelings of connectedness is nice, but if it doesn't shift our beliefs or practices, it isn't successful professional learning.

Beware artificial or ineffective collaboration

Teacher collaborative learning is not a panacea, and scholars warn about collaboration that is forced, insincere, and performative, rather than substantial (Hargreaves & O'Connor, 2018; Hargreaves & Shirley, 2009; Harris et al., 2018; Little, 1990). In teacher and school leader collaboration, norms of politeness and an absence of challenge can lead to collaboration that entrenches existing assumptions and practices. Little (1990) notes that teacher collaboration has been "imbued with a sense of virtue" (p. 509), but that it can in fact be "contrived, inauthentic, grafted on" (p. 510) or do more to "bolster isolation than to diminish it" (p. 511). Andy Hargreaves and Dennis Shirley (2009) warn against education reforms that are "data-driven and contrived" (p. 43), while Bob Garmston and Bruce Wellman (2013) similarly note that "conviviality and surface harmony mask underlying tensions and differences about the purposes and processes of teaching and learning" (p. 133). Peter Gronn (2003) warns against groupthink and coerced compliance. He encourages schools to guard against imposed collaborative groups that have such high degrees of attitudinal conformity that they are enslaved rather than empowered, and where learning, thinking, and decision making are actually impaired.

These warnings—against the surface appearance of harmony, masquerading as meaningful collaboration—are important ones for educators to consider. I have been a member of teams in which this kind of pretend collegiality was occurring. In more than one example I can recall, some members would sit silently during meetings, waiting for them to end. Then, after the meeting was finished, they would ignore, quietly undermine, or publicly criticise the decisions made by the team. The result is collaborative work that looks conflict-free on the surface, but that simmers with unexpressed resentment and frustration. This kind of team environment is toxic for the teachers and school leaders who are a part of it, and unhelpful for the organisation and students who are impacted by the work of the team. It is the result of putting colleagues in a room together, but without the necessary protocols, skills, and respect for effective collaboration to occur.

The importance of discomfort and dissent

Teachers harbour fears that rigorous collaboration lessens the individual latitude a person has and puts their preferences and practices under scrutiny by their peers (Little, 1990). I have worked in teaching teams in which student work is moderated after every assessment, but in which colleagues tell me privately that they worry about putting student work forward for fear that the group will override their decision to give a student a high mark. I have worked in teams in which some members deliberately isolate themselves so that their teaching practices, classroom layout, or lessons are not scrutinised (or criticised) by their peers. Collaboration can be scary, it can be uncomfortable, and it can result in teachers feeling that they are being coerced into doing things that go against the grain of their own beliefs about teaching or about the students they teach.

It may seem counterintuitive, but what collaborative teams need is the capacity to challenge one another and to work respectfully through discomfort and graceful disagreement. It may feel good to be part of a team that usually agrees and is positive in its interactions, but it is often through pushing back against one another that professional collaboration is most powerful. High-performing teams are not those who provide an echo chamber of group think, or whose members politely agree with one another, or always pat each other on the back for great ideas or a job well done. These behaviours might feel comfortable, but don't lead to the best work. The desire to avoid conflict can in fact undermine a group's purpose and work (Little, 1990). It is necessary in collaboration to have difficult conversations, productive conflict, collective responsibility, and peer accountability (Garmston & Wellman, 2013; Little, 1990). Effective collaboration needs skilful dissent and an environment in which it is ok to disagree.

The importance of collaborative norms

Time, money, and resourcing, advocated for in this book, are not sufficient to ensure effective professional learning or collaboration. What is additionally needed, especially in collaborative teams, is skill, effort, and effective structures to enable collaboration and learning. Some schools and systems work to address this need. For example, teachers involved in Ontario's Teacher Learning and Leadership Program participated in workshops on conflict resolution and adult learning (Lieberman et al., 2017). My own training in adaptive schools, various forms of coaching, and how to have difficult conversations, has helped me to bring protocols and structures to the collaborative partnerships and groups of which I have been a part.

Moving teachers' thinking from *my students* and *my work*, to *our students* and *our work*, requires clear purpose, safe structures, and collaborative inquiry around multiple sources of data (Lipton & Wellman, 2013). Bruce Tuckman's (1965) stages of group development provide a frame for professional collaboration. He outlines four stages of group development, commonly known as *forming* (orientation, testing one another, and developing dependencies), *storming* (a cathartic stage of conflict, polarisation, and emotional responses), *norming* (development of group cohesiveness, intimacy, and norms), and *performing* (purposeful high performance in which the group operates flexibly and optimally). An *adjourning* or termination phase was later added, in which a group disbands (Tuckman & Jensen, 1977).

What does collaborative professional learning look like?

The common goal of collaborative modes of professional learning is improved learning for students, via meaningful and ongoing learning for educators. Truly collaborative learning is about interdependent *joint work* that results in *collective action* (Little, 1990). Teacher collaborative learning is often based around data and evidence. More data, however, does not necessarily lead to better predictions (Garmston & Wellman, 2013), or to better practice. Learning communities work best when they set ambitious targets and high standards together, explore a wide range of mindful and meaningful questions, and become informed by statistical evidence and accumulated experience (Hargreaves & Shirley, 2009).

Collaboration can look like moderation marking meetings, less formal peer observation, collaboration over curriculum planning, interrogation of research literature in journal or book clubs, and a plethora of other collaborative practices. Those collaborative professional learning models for teachers and school leaders supported by research are:

- *Professional learning communities* (DuFour et al., 2017; Harris et al., 2018; Timperley et al., 2018);
- *Observation and reflection processes* such as *instructional rounds* (City et al., 2009), *quality teaching rounds* (Bowe & Gore, 2017); and *lesson study* (Cheung & Wong, 2014; Perry & Lewis, 2009; Takahashi & McDougal, 2016); and
- Developing school cultures of collaboration (Hargreaves & Fullan, 2012; Hargreaves & O'Connor, 2018).

Collaboration by teachers within schools can have a positive impact on student achievement; meanwhile, collaboration by teachers across schools can either lead to rich cross pollination of ideas and practices, or be fragmented and lack depth or sustainability (Carpenter & Linton, 2016). Depth and sustainability of professional learning are important if it is to have an impact on schools, teachers, and students; this is why in-school collaboration is worth pursuing. Within schools we are able to work closely, regularly, and on an ongoing basis, with our colleagues, under the umbrella of the school's shared vision and our shared commitment to our students. This allows depth of collaboration, and also its continuation and intensification over time. Collaboration is more than technical ways of collaborating; it is about building school cultures and systems in which individuals and schools work together for better outcomes.

On professional learning communities

It is worth spending some time teasing out the term *professional learning community*, or PLC, as the term is commonplace, but often misused in schools and discussions about education. The term 'PLC' has become so ubiquitous that it is used "ambiguously to describe virtually any loose coupling of individuals who share a common interest in education" and "is in danger of losing all meaning" (DuFour et al., 2017, p. 10). A PLC is not shorthand for a professional book club, or a team of teachers working together, or a group of teachers meeting in the same room meeting to collaborate superficially. Rather, it refers to a very specific model of teacher collaboration.

A PLC, according to Richard DuFour et al. (2017) is an iterative process of collective inquiry and action research, with an ongoing impact on the structure and culture of the school. Systematic and focused processes are required in order for PLCs to work, not only in the PLCs themselves, but also in the schools and systems within which teachers work (Timperley et al., 2018). A PLC that can be sustained over time is a collaborative group that has clarity about being a PLC, clarity about what model of PLC they are enacting, targeted support material, external expertise, and adequate resourcing (Harris et al., 2018). Louise Stoll and Karen Seashore Louis (2007) emphasise the PLC model as one that not only focuses on student learning and teachers' professional learning, but also on group cohesion, collective knowledge, and what they call "an ethic of interpersonal caring that penetrates the life of teachers, students, and school leaders" (p. 3). That is, PLCs are about more than the sum of their parts; they are based in a deep belief in the wellbeing of the people in schools and classrooms.

Alma Harris et al. (2018) point out that there have been many versions of the concept and multiple uses of the term PLC. They identify the following three categories of PLC models:

- *Whole school*, in which the entire school operates as a learning community with shared values and norms;
- *Within school*, in which collaborative groups or teams within a school take responsibility for leading research, improvement, and innovation; and
- *Across school*, in which teachers work collaboratively in a networked community with those at other schools.

Specifically, a PLC involves:

- A focus on high levels of student learning in which members constantly work to improve student results;
- A collaborative culture and collective responsibility in which members work interdependently for a shared purpose; and,
- A focus on results through a data-supported action research process based in evaluating evidence of student learning (DuFour et al., 2017).

Teachers in PLCs work together to maximise the learning of their students, and consider the students *our students* rather than *my students*. Collaboration is an expectation of all members of the PLC, who work "to achieve *common goals* for which members are *mutually accountable*" (DuFour et al., 2017, p. 12), founded in their shared mission, vision, values, and goals.

While DuFour et al. (2017) consider some aspects of a PLC flexible, or 'loose,' they consider the following elements to be non-negotiable or 'tight':

- Working collaboratively, taking collective responsibility for student learning, and making clear commitments to one another about how they will work together;
- The school being a collaborative team structure in which all members are mutually accountable;

- The team establishing a consistent curriculum so that all students have access to the same knowledge and skills no matter who their teacher is;
- The team developing common formative assessments to frequently gather evidence of student learning;
- The school creating a system of interventions and extensions to address student needs; and
- The team using evidence of student learning to inform and improve the individual and collective practice of its members.

These non-negotiables are intended to provide a frame within which teachers enact change. One foundational principle of PLCs is mutual accountability. When this works well, it means that all teachers see their goals as common and student learning as everyone's responsibility, students know that all members of the school community have both the same investment in student learning, and also the same expectations of students. Other basic beliefs in the PLC are that all students have equitable support in their learning and that consistent generation and use of evidence of student learning should inform and improve teaching practice. PLCs can develop teacher agency and efficacy, allowing teachers to solve their own problems of practice, but they need to be constantly willing to evaluate in what ways their efforts are making a difference (Timperley et al., 2018).

On lesson study

There are a number of instructional rounds models rounds (e.g. Bowe & Gore, 2017; City et al., 2009; Marzano, 2007). In instructional rounds a small network of teachers work collectively through a sustained inquiry process to enhance their teaching practice, based on classroom observation data. For Robert Marzano (2007), the main aim is for the observer to learn from other teachers and, through self-reflection and collaboration, apply this learning to their own teaching. While Marzano argues on the one hand that these observations are non-evaluative, he does suggest that observing teachers take notes on the positives and questions for each observed lesson segment, which some might argue is a form of evaluation.

Lesson study is one example of a kind of instructional round that involves teacher observation and collaboration. It originated in Japan as *jugyou* (lesson) *kenkyuu* (study) in the early 1900s, and has been the primary form of teacher professional learning in Japan for over a hundred years. Wai Ming Cheung and Wing Yee Wong (2014) report that lesson study has been found to have positive effects on students and teachers, including by increasing students' understanding of a subject and improving their learning efficiency. Sally Zepeda (2013) calls lesson study teacher-driven, classroom-based, job-embedded learning, grounded in data. Lesson study is focused on the improvement of teaching and learning practice in order to improve students' achievement, and involves teachers acting as researchers in order to plan, observe, and discuss together to produce and refine a research lesson. The research aspect of the lesson refers to the systematic process a group of teachers takes to design and observe a lesson around a particular topic or 'research theme.' There is no widely shared definition of 'research theme,' but it can be seen as encompassing a desired outcome for students, and an entry point for achieving that outcome (Takahashi & McDougal, 2016). The teachers' role in lesson study is active, collaborative, and systematic.

Lesson study has been described as a collaborative cycle of instructional improvement that involves collaborative goal setting around student learning; collaborative lesson planning; collaborative lesson investigation in which one team member teaches and others gather evidence on student learning; reflection on and discussion of the evidence gathered during the lesson; and consequent collaborative refinement of the lesson (Perry & Lewis, 2009). Akihiko Takahashi and Thomas McDougal (2016) also explain in detail the process Japanese teachers go through during the lesson study model:

> Japanese teachers begin lesson study by carefully reading the course of study, reading relevant research articles, and examining available curricula and other materials, a process called *kyouzai kenkyuu*, or 'study of materials for teaching' … They then design a lesson focused on a problematic topic while also addressing a broader research theme related to teaching and learning. This lesson, known as a 'research lesson' (*kenkyu jugyou*), is taught by a teacher from the planning team while the other team members—and other educators who are not on the planning team—observe. The planning team and observers then conduct a post-lesson discussion (*kenkyuu kyougikai*) focusing on how students responded to the lesson in order to gain insights into the teaching-learning process and into how the course of study should be implemented (p. 515).

In this way, lesson study gives teachers permission, time, and collaborative expertise to zero in on academic content, teaching materials, and pedagogical practice.

The Western world began to take notice of lesson study from the late 1990s, and it has recently become a more popular professional learning model around the world, including in the USA, the UK, Sweden, Hong Kong, Japan, Singapore, and Australia. It is a form of collaboration with a specific focus that allows teachers to share their expertise, observations, and questions in order to improve teaching and learning, as well as teacher efficacy and a sense of shared professional responsibility (Zepeda, 2013). Rebecca Perry and Catherine Lewis (2009) show that lesson study can be effectively used in the USA context, but add that there are a number of conditions necessary for lesson study to be effectively implemented. These conditions include establishing authentic professional communities; breaking down traditional hierarchical relationships and norms of private classroom practices; focusing on student thinking; and drawing on external knowledge sources.

In Japan, lesson study is historically and culturally embedded into teacher training and teaching as the primary mechanism for professional learning (Takahashi & McDougal, 2016). For Japanese teachers, lesson study is "like air, felt everywhere because it is implemented in everyday school activities, and so natural that it can be difficult to identify its critical and important features" (Fujii, 2014, p. 66); it is a fundamental part of teacher practice. Not only is it 'how we do things around here,' rather than a bolt-on, but it is part of a highly structured process shared at school or even district level. Toshiakira Fujii (2014) points out that many aspects of lesson study that are well understood by Japanese teachers have not transferred readily to contexts outside Japan. The approach has all the right ingredients, but—like all professional learning models—context matters, including the beliefs, attitudes, and experiences of teachers.

Spotlight on research: professional relationships are key to collaborative learning

While my PhD study did not look at a particular collaborative model such as PLCs or instructional rounds, participants discussed professional collaboration as a factor in their own professional learning. They discussed the importance of informal and collaborative aspects of learning, such as the interactions with fellow conference delegates, meetings with fellow action researchers, or working in ongoing teams such as faculty teams, teaching teams, pastoral teams, the coaching team, study groups, and collaborative action learning projects. Colleagues and students were seen as co-learners.

As discussed in Chapter 2, conferences and courses were seen by my PhD participants as opportunities for collaboration. Personal connections were often perceived as the most powerful aspect of those courses labelled 'professional development.' One teacher discussed a school-based action learning project as something that "reshaped" them. The project combined elements of self-choice and self-direction, with collaboration and expert consultation, resulting in changes to the teacher's approach to working with other teachers. They explained that, "That [project that occurred within the context of a collaborative group] has been, by far, the most powerful learning thing I've ever been through." One middle leader talked about a similar collaborative action research project that had the added layer of an online interactive journal that provided "a professional interaction about exploring ideas." The online journal was a place for the person to write their reflections, and for the facilitator of the learning group to add comments, in a kind of anytime online dialogue. For the leader, this collaboration was "extraordinary," providing a "high level of intellectual engagement" and "shared understanding" among the group and the group's expert facilitator. The online collaboration helped this leader to feel connected in with the facilitator, and to explore their thinking through writing that would receive feedback and interaction.

Research interviews, too, were found to be a site of learning through talking and listening. While not an obvious form of collaboration, these structured conversations were beneficial to both interviewer and interviewee. For me as researcher, interviewing school leaders was an opportunity to professionally learn from the stories of others. It was a privilege to hear the stories of the teachers and school leaders I interviewed for my PhD. While the point of the interviews was to generate data for analysis, a side effect was my own learning as I listened to—and through repeated data analysis—immersed myself in the experiences of other teachers and leaders. What was especially interesting for me was listening to the career and learning experiences, and beliefs and values, of the executive leaders.

Many of my school leader participants told me that the research interviews were sites of learning for them. They talked about the lack of time and space for reflection in their work days, and the way that the interview had allowed them the opportunity to verbalise it with an active listener. Being interviewed for this study was described by five leaders as a learning experience. They used words such as "a pleasure," a "privilege," and an "indulgence." One leader explained that the interview had given them "valuable" time and space to reflect upon their own educator self and leadership, thereby allowing them to think differently and in new ways; it was "the first time I thought of it like that." Another leader described the research interview as "very useful" as "there is so little time to reflect on what we do that I welcomed the opportunity in the form of the interview." One leader said, "You don't know the difference even doing this for me has made. It's an impact. I mean I've actually managed to think about my leadership style, that's wonderful." These reflections point towards the importance of time and reflection for teachers and school leaders to contemplate their work, identity, and professional purpose. So often meetings involve dissemination of information, or each individual waiting for their chance to speak. While there is little time allowed for it in many school settings, thinking out loud about teaching and leadership, and being really listened to, allows us to consolidate and develop our own thinking, and to connect with others.

The studied coaching intervention was a site of learning, partly because of the collaborative learning it facilitated. The interviewed teachers and I noted that our experience of the coaching intervention led to learning, especially through its combination of self-direction and collaboration. We noted that sites of learning included the team of teachers involved in the coaching intervention and the classrooms of teachers they observed. The teachers involved in the intervention were seen by each other as internal experts, educators from whom to learn. "What we're doing as a group," one teacher explained, "is we try and map out the best way of doing this. … we're mapping out the plan that's going to be followed to improve teacher quality in the future." This teacher felt that the intervention was doing important work. They enjoyed, even "loved," the reading, meetings, online discussions, and team work, elaborating that, when they had coaching intervention work on a given day, "you actually get up in the morning and you're looking forward to the day and I think that's important, too." School leaders also described the together-and-separate benefits of the coaching intervention as including the "extremely valuable deprivatising of practice" to hone "own teaching practice and share good teaching practice across the school."

Spotlight on practice: professional learning groups

In my whole school role of leading the professional learning—of about 140 teaching staff including those teaching Pre-Kindergarten all the way through to Year 12—I have wondered about how to develop a culture and structures of collaborative professional learning. In Chapter 8 I discuss my approach to my role, and the way in which my school has differentiated the internally offered professional learning pathways available to staff. This has given teachers and school leaders more voice and choice in the internal processes of professional learning in which they engage. Where before staff were allocated a school-based development process (such as coaching or manager evaluation) based on their place in a three-year cycle, in 2018 the school opened up a range of new options and each staff member negotiated with their line manager the one most appropriate to their career stage, interest and development needs. Each member of teaching staff is expected to engage in their own learning and development, knowing that no matter how good we each are, we can always be better, but the ways in which they go about this are more flexible and less rigid than the linear model the school has had in the past.

Here I discuss in more detail one of the offerings of the differentiated pathways model of professional learning: what we term professional learning groups or PLGs. These are groups of teachers coming together to share in their learning around a particular arena. These PLGs are opted in to by staff from a variety of year levels, from various faculties, and in a variety of roles. In 2018, its first year of implementation, 40 of our 140-odd teaching staff chose to be involved in one of these groups; each group included about ten people. In 2018, as an example, the following groups were on offer.

- *Effective classroom teaching.* Members of this group had a particular interest in teasing out classroom teaching. Participants came with a desire to reflect upon their core business of teaching, the needs of students in their classrooms, to share their own expertise with one another, and to read scholarly literature around pedagogy.
- *Pedagogies of learning spaces.* This group was made up of a range of teachers and leaders working in various learning spaces across the school, some of which were newly refurbished and some of which were well-established; each person's scenario came with its own individual circumstances. There was vibrant discussion and sharing of the practices, challenges, and benefits of co-teaching and teaching in open, flexible, inflexible, technology-rich, or technology-challenged spaces. These discussions were based in real practice, and in visits to each other's spaces.
- *ICT for teaching and learning.* Members of this group had a range of expertise and needs surrounding the use of technologies for teaching and learning. This made this the most challenging group; the very specific needs and very different expertise of each person meant that true collaboration around technologies was difficult. The decision was made to change this to a lunchtime club in 2019, with a specific calendar of skills building, software and hardware training, and hands-on workshops.
- *Postgraduate study.* My idea for this group came from my experience of doing a PhD. Working in a school while moonlighting as a postgraduate student can be incredibly isolating. There are often few people with which teachers and leaders can discuss study, especially self-directed research. This group was as much about solidarity, support, recognition and acknowledgement of those engaged in further study as it was about learning about research methods and research degrees. The members of this group were

those applying for postgraduate study, those in the throes of their higher degrees, and those nearing the end of their postgraduate degree. The breadth of experience meant that participants gained a lot from talking to, listening to, and learning from each. Interestingly, although this group was not re-offered in 2019, it is the one for which we have had the most requests from staff.

In 2019, these groups looked different; the focus areas shift as school strategy and staff professional needs develop and shift. Part of what feeds into this are data from staff about their professional learning needs and professional goals. In 2019, staff have themselves been proposing and negotiating professional learning groups that align with school strategy and team goals, while covering areas about which they are passionate.

As the recent Gonski 2.0 report (Gonski et al., 2018) noted, teachers would like time to talk about and collaborate around teaching. Groups like these can provide this opportunity. While from the outset I had a loose idea of what these groups would do—such as engage with research, reflect and workshop problems of practice together, share practice, visit one another's classrooms, collaborate in online spaces—I facilitate them in a way that allows the group's interests and needs to lead the way the group operates. This means employing structures for collaboration and coaching-style language, but in a way that is open to the groups working in ways that are unexpected or taking directions that are surprising. These are not groups in which I am the expert at the helm or the instructor imparting my knowledge. They are groups of expert practitioners whose value is in the rich expertise around the table, and the potential of professional conversation and collaboration about our daily work.

Each person has come to each group with a particular intention, and we fleshed these out in our first meetings. The opt in nature of the groups meant that staff generally arrived with enthusiasm for being involved; they have chosen this pathway for themselves. As my leadership role is Pre-Kindergarten to Year 12, and in a previous role I coached classroom teachers across the school around their classroom practice, I get to see the wonderful symbiotic connections between disparate areas of the school, but many staff do not have the opportunity to see the connections between themselves and others in the organisation. How might a Year 12 Design and Technology teacher know that their design thinking process mirrors that of the Pre-Primary classroom? What might be gained from connecting teachers using co-teaching pedagogies and flexible groupings in the Year 3 classrooms with those employing similar strategies in the Year 11 Physics course? The power of spending time with colleagues who share similar interests and challenges cannot be underestimated, especially in the environment of a large school where so often we can be siloed in our year level or faculty teams. There are benefits to those from vastly different areas of the school workshopping similar challenges and goals, ones they may not have known they shared with colleagues until coming together.

Teachers and school leaders need these kinds of professional learning opportunities that are at one self-chosen and self-directed, but also collaborative and supported. Professional communities are key to ensuring that change takes root and becomes part of the fabric of a school (Senge, 2012). Professional learning that happens on the school site is efficient, encourages staff collaboration, and has the potential to be sustained over time (Burstow, 2018). Often internal expertise goes unrecognised and untapped in schools. Looking outside and borrowing others' practice has its benefits, but schools can consider the expertise of those within their own walls, rather than looking to external experts. Teachers are experts in their own classrooms. School leaders are experts in their own schools.

Key takeaways

- Professional collaboration can benefit students and teachers, but needs to be deliberately designed around research-based principles and practices. Putting educators in a room together is not enough!
- Professional collaboration should be based on the clear shared purpose of improving outcomes for students, by developing teachers in meaningful and sustained ways.
- Key to collaborative professional learning are relationships, norms, protocols, processes, and data analysis that allow productive conflict, collective responsibility, and peer accountability. Getting along, enjoying the process, or patting each other on the back, does not equal collaboration.
- Examples of effective collaborative professional learning modes include professional learning communities, observation and reflection processes (such as instructional rounds and lesson study), moderation marking meetings, less formal peer observation, collaboration over curriculum planning, and interrogation of research literature in journal or book clubs.
- Within school and between school collaboration should be considered.

References

Bowe, J., & Gore, J. (2017). Reassembling teacher professional development: The case for Quality Teaching Rounds. *Teachers and Teaching, 23*(3), 352–366.

Burstow, B. (2018). *Effective teacher development: Theory and practice in professional learning*. London: Bloomsbury.

Carpenter, J. P., & Linton, J. N. (2016). Edcamp unconferences: Educators' perspectives on an untraditional professional learning experience. *Teaching and Teacher Education, 57,* 97–108.

Cheung, W. M., & Wong, W. Y. (2014). Does lesson study work?: A systematic review on the effects of lesson study and learning study on teachers and students. *International Journal for Lesson and Learning Studies, 3*(2), 137–149.

City, E. A., Elmore, R. F., Fiarman, S. E., & Teitel, L. (2009). *Instructional rounds in education: A network approach to improving learning and teaching*. Cambridge: Harvard Education.

Drago-Severson, E. (2012). *Helping educators grow: Strategies and practices for leadership development*. Cambridge: Harvard Education.

Drago-Severson, E., & Blum-DeStefano, J. (2018). *Leading change together: Developing educator capacity within schools and systems*. Alexandria: ASCD.

DuFour, R., DuFour, R., Eaker, R., Many, T. W., & Mattos, M. (2017). *Learning by doing: A handbook for professional learning communities at work* (3rd ed.). Moorabin: Hawker Brownlow Education.

Fujii, T. (2014). Implementing Japanese lesson study in foreign countries: Misconceptions revealed. *Mathematics Teacher Education and Development, 16*(1), 65–83.

Garmston, R. J., & Wellman, B. (2013). *Adaptive schools: A sourcebook for developing collaborative groups* (2nd ed.). Lanham: Rowman & Littlefield.

Gonski, D., Arcus, T., Boston, K., Gould, V., Johnson, W., O'Brien, L., … Roberts, M. (2018). *Through growth to achievement: The report of the review to achieve educational excellence in Australian schools.* Canberra: Commonwealth of Australia.

Gronn, P. (2003). *The new work of educational leaders: Changing leadership practice in an era of school reform.* London: Paul Chapman Publishing.

Hargreaves, A., & Fullan, M. (2012). *Professional capital: Transforming teaching in every school.* Moorabbin: Hawker Brownlow Education.

Hargreaves, A., & O'Connor, M. T. (2018). *Collaborative professionalism: When teaching together means learning for all.* Thousand Oaks: Corwin.

Hargreaves, A., & Shirley, D. (2009). *The fourth way: The inspirational future for educational change.* Thousand Oaks: Corwin.

Harris, A., Jones, M., & Huffman, J. B. (Eds.). (2018). *Teachers leading educational reform: The power of professional learning communities.* Abingdon: Routledge.

Lieberman, A., Campbell, C., & Yashkina, A. (2017). *Teacher leadership and learning: Of, by, and for teachers.* Abingdon: Routledge.

Lipton, L., & Wellman, B. M. (2013). *Learning-focused supervision: Developing professional expertise in standards-driven systems.* Charlotte: MiraVia.

Little, J. W. (1990). The persistence of privacy: Autonomy and initiative in teachers' professional relations. *Teachers College Record, 91*(4), 509–536.

Marzano, R. J. (2007). *The art and science of teaching: A comprehensive framework for effective instruction.* Alexandria: ASCD.

Perry, R. R., & Lewis, C. C. (2009). What is successful adaptation of lesson study in the US? *Journal of Educational Change, 10*(4), 365–391.

Senge, P. M. (2012). *Schools that learn: A fifth discipline fieldbook for educators, parents and everyone who cares about education* (2nd ed.). London: Nicholas Brearley.

Stoll, L., & Louis, K. S. (2007). *Professional learning communities: Divergence, depth and dilemmas.* Maidenhead: Open University Press.

Takahashi, A., & McDougal, T. (2016). Collaborative lesson research: Maximising the impact of lesson study. *ZDM Mathematics Education, 48*(4), 513–526.

Timperley, H., Ell, F., & Le Fevre, D. (2018). Developing adaptive expertise through professional learning communities. In A. Harris, M. Jones, & J. B. Huffman (Eds.). *Teachers leading educational reform: The power of professional learning communities* (pp. 175–189). Abingdon: Routledge.

Tuckman, B. W. (1965). Developmental sequence in small groups. *Psychological Bulletin, 63*(6), 384–399.

Tuckman, B. W., & Jensen, M. A. C. (1977). Stages of small-group development revisited. *Group & Organisation Management, 2*(4), 419–427.

Wenger, E. (2000). Communities of practice and social learning systems. *Organisation, 7*(2), 225–246.

Winnicott, D. W. (1960). The theory of the parent-infant relationship. *International Journal of Psychoanalysis, 41*(6), 585–595.

Zepeda, S. J. (2013). *Professional development: What works* (2nd ed.). New York: Routledge.

Chapter 5

Mentoring and coaching

This chapter works to separate the definitions and purposes of mentoring and coaching, exploring when and why each might be used, and coming to a clear understanding of what each entails. I thought long and hard about whether to put mentoring and coaching in the same chapter, as they are often unhelpfully conflated. Using the terms *mentoring* and *coaching* interchangeably does a disservice to both forms of professional learning and support. Here I delineate coaching from mentoring and provide clarity around what each is, and explore how and when each might be used in a professional learning context.

The chapter additionally presents a case study of one Australian school's coaching-for-professional-learning intervention. I reflect on my PhD research findings around coaching, and also reflect as a school leader who led a coaching-for-teacher-growth intervention through to completion, and the resulting shifts in language, practice, and culture at my school.

Mentoring: what, when, and why

While mentoring is a concept that has different meanings for different people in different places, it is generally understood as a one-to-one professional relationship between an experienced and a less experienced person for the purpose of learning or developing specific competencies (Murray, 2001). In a mentoring relationship there is a difference in experience and expertise, via the pairing of a master and a novice, with an expected imparting of knowledge from the more experienced mentor to the less experienced mentee. This can facilitate critical reflection, and help build mentees' confidence, professional agency, and capacity to view themselves as learners and professionals (Tonna et al., 2017). Mentoring is focused on promoting self-efficacy (Elliott et al., 2010). In education, as mentors are often subject specialists as well as expert teachers, they can help new teachers to develop their subject specialist teacher identity and practices (McIntyre & Hobson, 2016).

Mentoring tends to be focused on induction, support, and career transition. As evident in the recommendation of the recent Australian national review of teacher registration—"that teacher employers maintain responsibility and strengthen their role in providing access for early career teachers to high quality induction and mentoring, to support their transition into the workplace and the profession" (AITSL, 2018, p. iii)—mentoring is often seen as a way to support new teachers in their challenges entering the profession. It is also a way to help teachers stay in the profession (Heikkinen et al., 2018), thereby addressing teacher shortage and teacher turnover (Elliott et al., 2010). It has been suggested as a professional learning strategy for experienced teachers (Bressman et al., 2018) and also as a way to initiate new community members, spread expertise, transmit and reinforce organisational mission, and provide support to educators (Drago-Severson & Blum-DeStefano, 2018).

Hannu Heikkinen et al. (2018) point out the paradoxical nature of mentoring: that its dual purposes of acting *on* the mentee and of fostering communication *with* the mentee, are at odds with one another. This tension is evident in Elizabeth Elliott et al.'s (2010) recommendation that schools use on-site mentoring programs to closely monitor new teachers and introduce targeted strengths. Mentors can struggle to navigate the collaboration-control paradox; they grapple to find a way to be both controlling and not controlling, to ensure discipline while allowing collaboration, and to lead while also trusting others to lead. Mentoring works from the assumption that the mentee would benefit from someone else's expertise and so mentoring programs and relationships must navigate the complexities of the question: "Should mentees be regarded as autonomous individuals from the very beginning, or if not, where is the magic point at which the novices turn from heteronomous objects into autonomous subjects?" (Heikkinen et al., 2018, p. 10).

Mentoring and evaluation work best when they remain mutually exclusive as letting evaluation creep in to the mentoring relationship can have negative consequences (Bressman et al., 2018). The vulnerability of the mentee is apparent in Joanna McIntyre and Andrew Hobson's (2016) finding that mentees often feel they cannot divulge real professional learning needs to mentors from within their own schools, for fear of being judged as inadequate. Michelle Tonna et al. (2017) warn that "if mentors do not provide sufficient challenge, the relationship can easily change into a situation where the mentees shift responsibility for their anxieties and problems onto the mentor" (p. 219). Mentors themselves face challenges. In education, teachers are often tapped on the shoulder to be mentors because they are excellent teachers, but being a mentor requires a different set of skills and often requires building a different kind of identity as a recognised expert and an outsider to others' classrooms (Lieberman et al., 2017). There can be pressure on mentors as their role is to facilitate the improvement of the mentee's teaching.

Sometimes a mentoring relationship is an informal one, rather than one formalised by observations of practice and regular meetings; mentors find us or we find them. Trust is key in these relationships; they cannot be manufactured. Participants in my PhD study described mentors who had shaped them. One executive leader talked about two "remarkable" principals who gave this leader "incredible" early-on leadership opportunities and "the confidence to take a next step" through saying "you're good enough to do this." Being "believed in" empowered and buoyed this leader. A personal example for me is from the early years of my teaching career. At 23 years old and with little experience in leading teams, I was promoted into a leadership role as head of middle school English. I consider my line manager from that time as a mentor. I would often ask for advice on a student, parent, or staffing issue. While this was close to 20 years ago, I remember how welcome I felt in her office, and how safe the space was. She would put everything else aside, listen intently to me, and then move between helping me generate my own ideas, and advising me based on her own experience and expertise.

Now, there are colleagues who arrive at my office door, seeking for me to listen, to collaborate, or to advise. I am influenced in my response to those colleagues by those leaders who I admire, those mentors to whom I have looked up, and also by my coaching training that has emphasised the importance of trust and rapport, and helps me to see everyone as having the capacity to solve their own problems. I always put aside what I am doing if someone arrives at my door. I welcome them, invite them to sit, ask them how they are, and wait for them to speak. In the beginnings of the conversation especially, this is a time for them to work through what they have come to say or explore, a confidential space to articulate fears, concerns, or aspirations.

Coaching: what, when, and why

Mentoring tends to be focused on induction, support, and career transition, while coaching focuses on knowledge creation and improving practice (Fletcher, 2012). Unlike the mentor-mentee relationship of master-novice, the coach-coachee relationship may be peer-to-peer, or with a coach who is expert in coaching, but not necessarily an expert in the work of the coachee.

Coaching is another term with multiple definitions and uses. In my experience, coming to a shared definition is challenging. Research presents contradictory notions of coaching; speakers on coaching at conferences each bring a different lens to their presentations; and in a school or education system environment, individuals and groups bring their own assumptions about, and lived experiences of what they consider to be, 'coaching.' Some people think of sports coaching, in which an expert guides individuals or team to develop their skill, through providing skill analysis, skill development, and motivation. Some people conflate the notion of mentoring with coaching, despite these being very different models of learning, with dissimilar roles and purposes. Some have described coaching in education as in-service professional learning in which coaches observe teachers' instruction and provide feedback to help them improve (Kraft et al., 2016), but the notion of providing feedback is contested and slippery in coaching. What kind of feedback is appropriate? How does the coach resist their own impulses to fix or advise, and instead coach the coachee into self-directedness?

Coaching develops the coachee's self-efficacy (Rhodes & Fletcher, 2013), practice, agency, and leadership capacity (Charteris & Smardon, 2014). Coaches do not provide advice and solutions, but provoke thinking and provide space for reflection (Charteris & Smardon, 2014). Coaching can be practised in a way that counteracts the performativity agenda in schools, while still existing within that context (Lofthouse, 2019). School leaders can be uncomfortable with the notion of teachers identifying their own development priorities and may be tempted to disguise performance management as coaching thereby undermining its intent (Munro et al., in press). Andy Hargreaves and Jane Skelton (2012) warn about cultures in which coaches force compliance rather than helping teachers help themselves to build capacity.

They caution that while coaching may originate as "a learning journey taken by travellers together" (p. 135), it has often, within the context of large scale systematic reform, become enforced, done *to* people for the purposes of compliance with externally prescribed practice.

Coaching's moral purpose is to develop professional capacity, professional capital, and productive humanity. John Whitmore's (2009) definition of coaching as "unlocking people's potential to maximise their own performance" (p. 10) reflects the metaphor of the stagecoach, which reminds us that coaching is about getting the coachee from where *they* currently are to where *they* want to be (not to where the coach wants them to be, and not to where management wants them to be).

My definition of coaching is as follows:

Coaching is a collaborative process by which a coach acts as mediator, mirror, and conduit for the coachee's own thinking, in order to develop self-directedness and self-efficacy, and to move the coachee towards an improvement or solution that is owned by them.

This process involves the eking out of the coachee's thinking, rather than telling. It requires conversation maps or structures, including ways to effectively begin and conclude coaching conversations; deliberate conversational behaviours such as eye contact and mirroring or open body language; a lot of listening, pausing, and paraphrasing; and asking well-crafted questions designed to engage with the coachee's thinking. Coaching is underpinned by a belief in the coachee's capacity to learn, grow, and come up with their own ideas and solutions. One of my biggest learnings as a coach is that coaching often means keeping myself—my own assumptions, ideas, solutions, and curiosities—out of the conversation, and being fully present for the coach and what they need. When I am coaching it is not at all about me, or even my expertise, but entirely about the coachee. I am, as the above definition suggests, mediator, mirror, and conduit.

In an education context, coaching can improve teaching and teachers' experiences of professional learning (Lofthouse et al., 2010). Jon Andrews and Chris Munro (2019) describe coaching as an "intricate agency-building process that cuts to the heart of being professional, feeling valued and heard, and worthy of trust and respect" (p. 170). Coaching teachers has positive effects on teacher instructional practice and on student achievement (Kraft et al., 2016). It may also indirectly benefit those with whom the coachee interacts, such as students or staff, as the coachee may become a coach for others (Rhodes & Fletcher, 2013). In my PhD research, I found that the ramifications of coaching radiated out from the coaches and coachees to influence other people and norms within the organisation and beyond it (Netolicky, 2016).

Simply being trained in coaching skills and following a coaching process do not, however, guarantee successful coaching outcomes (van Nieuwerburgh, 2017). Coaches themselves need ongoing support in order to work through challenges and be deeply reflective about coaching practice.

Types of coaching in education contexts

While many agree that coaching is a valuable form of professional learning that impacts positively on thinking and practice, the most effective models and ideological approaches are in dispute. The term *coaching* describes a variety of models in which teachers are paired with a coach for a variety of purposes. Some researchers have attempted to group coaching into areas. See, for instance, the seminal work of Beverley Showers and Bruce Joyce (1996) who identify peer coaching, cognitive coaching, technical coaching, team coaching, and collegial coaching; or Jake Cornett and Jim Knight (2008) who identify peer coaching, cognitive coaching, literacy coaching, and instructional coaching.

Instructional coaching (Cornett & Knight, 2008) claims to see coach and coachee as equal, dialogic, and reciprocal partners. The teacher's professional knowledge and experience is acknowledged, but so is the instructional coach's knowledge of 'evidence-based teaching practices.' Instructional coaching involves gathering and reviewing lesson data, goal setting, the suggesting and explaining of evidence-based teaching practices by the coach; the coach modelling the new practice; and the teacher practising the new practice while more data is generated (Knight & van Nieuwerburgh, 2012). Instructional coaching was found to increase the frequency and quality of uptake of new classroom practices, when compared with teachers who do not receive coaching support (Cornett & Knight, 2008). Instructional coaching seems to lean towards what might be termed *consulting*, which involves an expert in teaching offering information, ideas, expertise, and analysis, often based on the assumption that the teacher lacks the necessary information or ideas to move their practice forward (as per the definition of consulting provided by: Costa & Garmston, 2015; Lipton & Wellman, 2013). Some suggest that coaching remain separate from any kind of evaluation, including judgements and advice (Showers & Joyce, 1996).

Peer coaching, a non-evaluative, non-hierarchical form of coaching (Zepeda et al., 2013), appeared in education literature in the 1980s. Bruce Joyce and Beverley Showers (1988) define the main purpose of peer coaching as the implementation of innovations in order to effect positive change for students—the essential aim for any professional learning in schools! They assert that coaching builds: collaborative teaching communities; shared language and understandings; clearer cognition of teaching purpose and practice; and collegial and experimental school norms that support continuous teacher improvement and school change. Allowing teachers to observe and learn from each other stimulates the sharing of knowledge, while the giving of feedback shapes aspiration towards and language of quality instruction, and develops a positive learning culture among teachers. The positive effects of peer coaching are supported by Kenneth Wong and Anna Nicotera (2003). In their synthesis of literature, they found that peer coaching can promote a culture of collaboration and professionalism, while expanding teachers' working repertoires of planning and instructional strategies.

Some studies have found elements of peer coaching problematic. For example, Suleyman Goker (2006) found peer coaching promoted confidence, autonomy, and self-directed learning. However, his work also revealed a primary concern of peer coaching: it relies on teachers' capacities for self-reflection and self-directed development. Goker's participants had a lack of a language of reflection, difficulty being self-critical, and difficulty identifying strategies for improving practice. This points to a potential criticism of peer coaching: while providing a safe environment for teacher growth, peer coaching does not provide the kind of expert feedback of the instructional coaching or consulting model which might add to a teacher coachee's repertoire of knowledge and skills. Other problems identified with peer coaching include scheduling, weak peer partners, the lack of skills to provide effective feedback, time constraints, and increased workload (Zepeda et al., 2013).

Additionally, a tension can arise in school peer coaching contexts when school leaders colonise and infiltrate the process for monitoring and organisational agendas, rather than protecting it as a collaborative learning process (Lofthouse & Leat, 2013; Lofthouse et al., 2010). In context and in practice, peer coaching, like other forms of professional learning, can have "a troubled identity, caught between empowerment and managerialism" (Lofthouse & Leat, 2013, p. 9), in which school leaders are perceived to be exercising control over teacher learning. This concern of the potential corruption of the initially good intentions of a teacher coaching program was one that surfaced in my PhD study; some participants were worried that the school would eventually allow coaching to be a performance management tool to surveil teachers or call them to account, rather than a trusted space for professional reflection and development.

Cognitive coaching (Costa & Garmston, 2015), the model of coaching used in the school I studied for my PhD, is a form of coaching that can be conducted by an expert or peer. It bases its approach on the understanding that neuro-chemical pathways in the brain work in such a way that if an individual does not feel safe, they cannot think and learn. According to Art Costa and Bob Garmston (2003), "if threat, fear, pain even in the most minute portions are perceived, neurological and chemical processes occur which prepare the system for survival, not reflection" (p. 5). While for learning to occur, there may be what Costa and Garmston (2003) call "disequilibrium," or what Rachel Lofthouse et al. (2010) call "rethinking" or "dissonance," there needs to be a foundation of safety and trust for thinking and reflection to occur. This reflects subsequent research that looked at neural responses to different types of coaching, which found that coaching that emphasises compassion has been shown to positively enhance openness to learning and incite behavioural change, while deficiency-based coaching for compliance results in defensiveness and reduced cognitive functioning (Boyatzis et al., 2013; Jack et al., 2013).

Reading the work of Richard Boyatzis et al. (2013) and Anthony Jack et al. (2013) was an 'a-ha' moment for me in my own coaching journey. As a teacher and school leader I was always keen to be helpful somehow. This often meant that I did a lot of work in conversations in which I tried to think of advice or solutions for students and staff. What I realised was that when the individual does their own thinking, and comes up with their own solutions, not only is it developing their efficacy, but it is more helpful in the short and long term, and more likely to be enacted or to make a difference.

Cognitive coaching actively discourages specific feedback or advice from the coach to the coachee, positive or negative. It focuses instead on the coachee's cognition and capacity for self-reflection, goal setting, and growth. Its goal is developing both self-directed individual learners and the individual's interdependence with the school system (Costa & Garmston, 2015). While four roles are available to the cognitive coach—coach, collaborator, consultant, and evaluator—the default role is of the coach: non-judgemental mediator of cognition. This approach is intended to create personal change through new connections in the brain; reconstructing knowledge through a conscious, reflective approach to new experiences. Inner thought processes are targeted, rather than outer behaviours (Batt, 2010; Costa & Garmston, 2015). A cognitive coaching approach would argue that even positive feedback is evaluative feedback, inhibiting the teacher's thinking. Coaching that facilitates coachee self-efficacy and solving of own problems of practice aligns with Dylan Wiliam's (2014) suggestion that the teacher choose the foci for their improvement, that "each teacher has a better idea of what will improve the learning of their students, in their classroom, in the context of what they are teaching them, than anyone else" (p. 33).

Some research supports cognitive coaching as an effective change agent for teachers. Jennifer Edwards and Ray Newton's (1995) quasi-experimental study of 143 teachers over two years found that it increased teachers' use of higher level questions, feelings of efficacy, and feelings of satisfaction with teaching as a career. Ellen Batt's (2010) study of 15 elementary teachers found that cognitive coaching had a direct effect on teachers' practice and that teachers found the coaching process worth the time spent. Teachers in Batt's study attributed shifts in their own perceptions of teaching and learning, and gains in student achievement, to coaching. The use of a cognitive coaching process for teacher capacity building is supported by Charlotte Danielson's (2007) caution that mentors, supervisors, evaluators, and colleagues beware of imposing their own styles or preferences when observing.

In my own experience of cognitive coaching—as someone who has completed the cognitive coaching foundation course three times and experienced it as a coach and coachee for seven years—cognitive coaching has power to shift thinking, beliefs, and practices. It also has its limitations, and can be frustrating for the coachee when they feel stuck in their thinking, and desire more directive advice or a more collaborative approach to problem solving by the coach. This is where Laura Lipton and Bruce Wellman's (2013) continuum of interaction is useful in navigating appropriate approaches to professional conversation, including when and why to coach, collaborate, consult, calibrate, or evaluate.

More recently I have added GROWTH coaching (Campbell, 2016) to my coaching toolkit. The GROWTH model gives leaders and coaches an accessible framework to apply to goal setting and coaching conversations. It additionally sets up the notion of coaching as a *way of being* (van Nieuwerburgh, 2017) and of the power of informal corridor coaching conversations, which suggest that schools can build cultures permeated by coaching as a way of listening, communicating, and reflecting.

Spotlight on research: researching a school coaching model

My PhD was based around the context of a school coaching model, an intervention designed to develop the professional culture of the school, professional conversations, reflection around teaching practice, and an improvement in teaching via this professional learning and growth of teachers. In 2012 I was charged with implementing a school-based model that used short lesson observations with the coach-observer taking low inference data, cognitive coaching, and the Danielson Framework for Teaching. The specifics of the model—what it looked like and how it was implemented at the school—is described next in the spotlight on practice. What I explain here in the spotlight on research is what my PhD study found about the impact on teachers of this in school coaching model.[1]

My PhD data revealed that cognitive coaching training and practice impacted those teacher participants involved in the coaching intervention as coaches and coachees. The teacher participants and I reflected that what was most helpful to teachers in growing their practice was mediating thinking rather than giving advice. This model used the Danielson Framework for Teaching as a tool to develop a language of reflection and a common understanding of what good teaching looks like, and participants noted that the coaching intervention team began to use the language of the Danielson Framework for Teaching, and cognitive coaching ways of being and speaking, within and beyond the context of the coaching model.

The coaching work—in which, during the pilot phase, we were all coaches and coached by each other—incited the teachers and I to reconsider the role and purpose of a coach. I noted in a research interview that it "affected how I speak to people whether it's my students, my colleagues, my friends, or my own kids." For me, coaching became a way of being, "a part of the way you talk and how you approach conversation whether in a classroom, a team, or personal relationships." So our involvement in the coaching intervention influenced our conversations with students in classrooms, in our collaborative teaching teams, in meetings with parents and managers, and in our personal and family relationships.

The teacher-as-coach model was felt by these participants to be important, confirming that the relationship must be safe, confidential, and non-evaluative and that coaching relationships in which there is hierarchical imbalance or evaluation may be counter-productive. The coach-coachee relationship was seen by participants, including school leaders, as a key to professional growth, affirming that trust and credibility in the coaching relationship are keys to productive open conversations.

Although school leaders participating in this study saw the coaching intervention as positively shifting the professional culture of the school, two school leaders had some questions around what they saw as a potentially uncontrolled approach to professional learning. One middle leader wondered about the possibility that "it could be too self-directed ... or even peer-directed." That is, that leaders would be left out of the process of working alongside and guiding their staff, or that individual teachers would be without the tools and help they need to improve. This reflects Goker's (2006) concerns about the limits of coaching and incites the question of whether leaders are able to operate from the belief that teachers have the capacity to know their own students and classrooms, and to solve their own problems of practice. This leader's comment suggests that leaders can be skeptical and questioning of professional learning approaches that give teachers autonomy. Another middle leader worried that the intervention may "morph over time," straying from its original purpose or "being corrupted" by strategic or administrative pressures. This leader's concerns reflect the concerns of many working in schools about the corruption of the often good intentions of education reform into evaluative or punitive mechanisms to constrain rather than develop teachers.

School leaders in my PhD study talked about their own experiences of coaching as professional learning. Conversations with coaches provided safe, trusted places for this study's participants to learn, grow, think, and reflect. Five leaders discussed formal and informal coaching relationships as important learning for them. Four executive leaders talked about formal coaching relationships, organised by themselves or by the school, as spaces in which they could explore their leadership in a safe and challenging environment. These trusting and self-chosen relationships helped them to develop their teaching and leading and gave them a space to safely explore work problems. The school leaders and I learned through talk and conversation, experiences which we reflected brought our thinking to the surface and extended it. One executive leader explained that having a coach has developed their "own self" and "conscious awareness" of "what I am good at" as well as "where I should look at spending more chunks of my time." Conversations with a professional coach have helped to develop the leader's "openness," "consciousness," and self-awareness, while giving them the space to explore and work through school leadership problems.

Issues remain of the effects of hierarchical relationships on the individual, and the possibility of performative teaching-to-the-observation, rather than authenticity in observed lessons. These issues have implications for who might be the best person to coach teachers in their practice when growth and positive change are the aims. Coachees might be best served by coaches who are not also their managers, as unequal power and managerial authority is potentially damaging for the coaching relationship. If the purpose of a school-based coaching intervention is teacher professional growth and improvement in practice, as with the coaching intervention, then coaching should not be conflated with evaluation, performance management, mentoring, or consultation.

In these ways, my PhD study confirms other research findings in the coaching literature such as the importance of trust, the need to protect the coaching relationship as a safe and confidential space, and the potential of coaching for positive learning and culture building. It additionally found that being a coach can be an empowering and identity shaping experience, that coaching for empowerment and capacity building benefits from a non-hierarchical relationship, that coaching can be enhanced by the use of additional tools and approaches, and that a coaching intervention can have unexpected nonlinear butterfly effects beyond the model itself (Netolicky,

2016). Coaching in this school context was found to be an identity shaping experience with unexpected and far reaching impacts, demonstrating that the combination of being a coach and coachee can facilitate empowerment, professional growth, and changes in belief and practice.

Spotlight on practice: implementing a school-based coaching model

In August 2012 I presented a paper to the school board around the then-popularised concept of teacher quality and quality instruction. This included ways to build teacher capacity, how this sat with the context of our school, and the beginning of a proposed approach to the development of a pilot project in developing teaching and teachers at my school. In the conversation that initiated the studied coaching intervention at my school, I asked the principal, "What do you want the end point to be?" and the principal said, "I want to develop the learning culture of the staff." The principal added that they wanted the school and staff room to be places of vibrant professional conversation; deprivatised classrooms with open doors in which teachers welcomed each other in; and willingness to be professionally vulnerable, learn from one another, and reflect deeply on teaching practice in order to improve it. This notion of an energetic, collaborative, and open professional learning culture, developed via coaching as professional learning, resonates with Christian van Nieuwerburgh and Jonathan Passmore's (2012) description of a school-wide coaching culture for learning as one in which coaching "is used consistently by all partners across the school community, to help develop learning, understanding and personal responsibility in others from staff, to parents and from students to governors and wider stakeholders" (p. 159). Helen Gormley and Christian van Nieuwerburgh (2014) explain that

> a coaching culture exists within an organisation when it has embedded a coaching approach as part of its strategic plans in a transparent way. Coaching cultures should motivate individuals and facilitate cooperation, collaboration, and connection within the organisation and with its external stakeholders (p. 99).

So, the coaching intervention—planned in 2012, piloted in 2013 and 2014, and fully implemented from 2015—was about more than individual teachers and their students benefiting from coaching. It was more broadly about organisational culture and the teachers at the school as a high functioning collective.

Across the two years of the pilot intervention—2013 and 2014—there were 19 teacher coaches and 11 official teacher coachees (although there were others who were coached on a more informal basis as part of coaches' training and practice). These teachers came from across the Pre-Kindergarten to Year 12 school and from multiple faculties.

The teacher coaches spent their time in the following ways:

- Being trained and immersed in the Danielson Framework for Teaching and cognitive coaching;
- Participating at various levels in several types of classroom observations and coaching conversations, including as observed coachee and observer coach;
- Working in sub-committees to develop plans and resources for data generation and analysis, human resources processes and documentation, alignment of the coaching model with national standards and expectations, and developing clear maps of and protocols for the model to be implemented;
- Meeting as a collegial, open-minded, and critically thinking team to discuss, develop, refine, and evaluate the tools, protocols, and processes of the project;
- Participating in focus groups to feed back experiences, ideas, and lessons learned; and
- Regularly utilising online discussion forums as an extension of face to face meeting time.

Below, I outline the details of this particular coaching model, which was designed with this school context in mind. I also share an overview of the work involved in rolling out this model in the appendices (see Table A.1). This outline is not intended as a blueprint for success in other schools, but as one example of a contextually-relevant school-based approach to coaching as professional learning.

The trial model

The trial coaching model was a yearly cycle that was intended to facilitate teachers' reflection on specific data from their classroom practice, with the support of a teacher coach. The coaches were called 'teacher coaches' as they were all teachers who had no positional responsibility. This was a deliberate decision in order to preserve the trust within the coach-coachee relationship.

The yearly coaching cycle involved the following steps:

- *Teacher coachee self-reflection* against the Danielson Framework for Teaching.
- *Preconference* with teacher coach. This initial conversation was to touch base, identify possible foci for lesson observations and coaching, and decide on type of lesson data to be collected. The foci and data were generated from the teacher coachee around what would be meaningful for them.
- *Two 20-minute lesson observations* including data generation.
- *Post conference* with the teacher coach. This post-observations conversation followed the cognitive coaching reflecting-into-planning conversation map and used the Danielson Framework for Teaching as a self-reflective tool in which teachers could place their lessons against the descriptors.

Then, the previous two steps were repeated (lesson observations plus post conference coaching conversation).

Short lesson observations with low inference data

As can be seen from the steps of the yearly coaching cycle, generating lesson data was a crucial part of this coaching intervention. While all data have their inherent biases, benefits, and disadvantages, this model used multiple short observations and the Danielson Framework for Teaching, as supported by the findings of the Measures of Effective Teaching study (Kane & Staiger, 2012). A number of short observations—often of different kinds of lessons or parts of lessons—meant that teachers built up a series of snapshots of the kinds of lessons in their classrooms, liberating them from feeling like 'this 20 minutes is representative of all of my teaching all of the time.' That is, observations represented a moment in time on which to reflect.

While all teachers were expected to have data generated in their lessons, the collecting of this data was differentiated in the sense that the teacher coachee decided what sort of data would be collected, depending on what they wanted to reflect upon in their teaching. Lesson data were low inference—that is, as close to factual or objective information (rather than opinion or evaluation)—as possible. The following types of lesson data were generated.

- *Non-inferential observation notes, often verbatim scripting.* The teacher coach would record what they see and hear in a lesson without judgements, praise, or criticism. Coaches were trained in this kind of observational note taking, which is useful for looking at instructional clarity, questioning, student discussion, and student group or individual work. In the case of the latter, the observer would go to students or groups and observe them or interact with them, recording interactions and responses. This meant that often coaches could record those parts of the classroom where teachers were not. The benefit of written or typed notes is that the run of the lesson is down in black and white, without the distractions of watching multiple elements in a video.
- *Video,* whether taken on stationary cameras, smart phones, or tablets. Different video technologies offered different pros and cons, such as whose audio is picked up and whose movement is tracked. The choice depends on if the teacher wants to focus on themselves, their instruction, their language, their movement, and their wait times; or on the language, movement, and behaviours of their students. Video was an effective way for teachers to see their own teaching, including movement and wait times.
- *Audio,* which allowed teachers to reflect on what was said in their classrooms. Audio recording allowed teachers to listen closely to their questioning and their students' responses. Sometimes these were additionally transcribed.
- *Supplementary data* including planning documents, goals, and reflections, student work samples, student feedback, and student achievement data.

Importantly, these data were all requested and 'owned' exclusively by the teacher for their reflection and use. They were not for coaches to use or publicise outside of the teacher-coach relationship.

Focus groups with coached teachers revealed that teachers appreciated the choice and ownership over their classroom data. Mixing the data up seemed to allow teachers to focus on different things in subsequent coaching cycles. As a coach myself during the pilot years of the model, I found that when we got the data right, the conversation seemed to almost take care of itself. The data, in some cases, set off a teacher's thinking, reflection, planning, and action before I turned up for the post conference. In other conversations, looking at the data in detail, with well-crafted questions, brought teachers to the point of an 'a-ha' moment or a change in practice. Lesson data itself could be transformational.

Lessons learned

As leader of the coaching intervention, I used anonymous surveys and focus groups of coaches and coachees to gain insights into the impacts of the coaching intervention. These school data revealed that the coaching of teachers in this way: helped to build relationships between teachers across the school; incited and shaped professional conversation and reflection; shifted professional culture to one more accepting of reflection and use of lesson data to inform teaching and learning; and developed a shared language around teaching and what 'good' teaching might look like.

Coaches generally found the work of coaching interesting, professionally meaningful, and even transformational. The Danielson Framework for Teaching provided a common language and shared understandings of what good teaching is and how it looks in a classroom. Cognitive coaching provided an approach to professional conversations that allowed the teacher to do the thinking and developing of their own practice. The main concern of coaches was around logistical and time constraints. Many struggled to find appropriate times to observe and chat to their teacher coachees due to conflicting timetables. Coaches were especially concerned when these challenges resulted in a long time between lesson observations and the follow-up conversation.

For teachers, the experience was generally described as positive, meaningful, useful, and unobtrusive. Their own reflections, conclusions, and goals were made; they felt they owned the process. There were some inconsistencies in teacher experiences; some found it more or less helpful than others; some found their coaches to be more effective than others; at least one seemed disappointed by their coach. One of the things teachers most appreciated was the building of a collegial relationship with the coach and this process as a catalyst for professional dialogue and connections. In a few cases the coaching cycle led to other conversations and a closer professional relationship. Teachers felt that coaches were able to draw insights and reflections they would have been unable to generate for themselves. Teachers expressed a desire to have some ownership over the coaching partner. They agreed that perhaps being able to choose anyone they would *not* want to work with might be a good solution. The comfort with a coach was related to teachers' feeling that they needed a positive, safe relationship with their coach in order to be vulnerable.

The continuous nature of the cycle allowed coaches and coachees to see growth. Teachers felt their familiarity with the Danielson Framework for Teaching and their ability to ask for meaningful data, and reflect on it, developed over time. Different teachers found different kinds of data useful but all appreciated being able to decide what data was taken in their lessons. There was some reflection around the one-sided nature of the coach-teacher relationship where the teacher would have liked more engagement or involvement from their coach partner in order to feel that they had a collegial relationship.

The need for trust within the coaching relationship is paramount. Coaching needs to be based in pursuing a growth-focused culture of continuous improvement in which members are self-directed, self-efficacious, and agentic. This means that coaching needs to be separated out from evaluative or performance review processes and not be used as a deficit model aimed to 'fix' or improve teachers. There is a need to navigate and consider the balance or imbalance of positional authority in coach-coachee relationships. When the coach-coachee relationship involves a coach being a teacher and the coachee a manager, or the coach a manager and the coachee a person with less organisational power, the openness of the conversation and the learning that is possible are hindered. When I have been coached by someone higher up the organisational hierarchy, I have found myself thinking carefully about what I should or shouldn't talk about with that person, meaning that the coaching conversation can become contrived or guarded, rather than open and useful in its purpose of serving the coachee. This kind of 'impression management' for fear of being judged undermines the purpose of coaching (Munro et al., in press). Effective coaching conversations are based in relational trust and rapport, and in the coach believing in the capacity and capability of the coachee.

Finally, coaching was not the only professional learning opportunity on offer at the school. There were processes for induction, probation, evaluation, and collaboration, as well as a variety of internal and external professional development opportunities. The coaching model was rolled out to all staff in 2015. Then, since 2017, we have worked towards a differentiated model of in-house professional learning in which staff have voice and choice in taking advantage of a process that most suits their career stage and needs, including those in or aspiring to leadership positions. These options, discussed in the spotlight on practice in Chapter 8, include different types of coaching by different types of coaches, and also more advisory, mentor-style relationships, and collaborative groups that run like PLCs or journal clubs.

Key takeaways

- Mentoring is a one-to-one professional relationship between an experienced and a less experienced person for the purpose of learning or developing specific competencies. In education it is usually focused on induction, support, and career transition.

- Coaching is a collaborative process by which a coach acts as mediator, mirror, and conduit for the coachee's own thinking, in order to develop >self-directedness and self-efficacy, and to move the coachee towards an improvement or solution that is owned by them.
- Mentoring and coaching (and other support processes such as consulting, collaborating, and evaluating) should not be conflated. Rather a school or system should have a very clear shared understanding about what is meant by these terms.
- As always, context matters. Schools need to look to and start from their own contexts. They can ask: Where are our staff, students, and community at? What do we want from coaching? How do we move towards a coaching culture in a way that best suits our community and our needs? A coaching model should not be lifted from one school and onto another.
- Coaching is not a stand-alone solution or silver bullet. It can be useful as a key part of a suite of professional learning opportunities within schools.
- Introducing and using coaching as an approach to professional conversation can influence the culture of that organisation, but equally, pre-existing organisational conditions make a successful and vibrant coaching culture possible (or difficult). Organisational conditions for coaching include *organisational trust* (e.g. that the leadership team aren't going to corrupt the intention of coaching or undermine the confidentiality of the coaching relationship) and *semantic space* where coaching becomes a 'way we talk around here.'

Note

1 It is worth noting that this coaching intervention was not a stand-alone solution, but part of a suite of professional learning opportunities, including those that were more directed, content-based, or expert-driven.

References

Andrews, J., & Munro, C. (2019). Coaching for agency: The power of professionally respectful dialogue. In D. M. Netolicky, J. Andrews, & C. Paterson (Eds.). *Flip the system Australia: What matters in education* (pp. 163–171). Abingdon: Routledge.

Australian Institute for Teaching and School Leadership (AITSL). (2018). *One teaching profession: Teacher registration in Australia*. Carlton South: Education Council.

Batt, E. G. (2010). Cognitive coaching: A critical phase in professional development to implement sheltered instruction. *Teaching and Teacher Education, 26*(4), 997–1005.

Boyatzis, R. E., Smith, M. L., & Beveridge, A. J. (2013). Coaching with compassion: Inspiring health, well-being, and development in organisations. *The Journal of Applied Behavioural Science, 49*(2), 153–178.

Bressman, S., Winter, J. S., & Efron, S. E. (2018). Next generation mentoring: Supporting teachers beyond induction. *Teaching and Teacher Education, 73*, 162–170.

Campbell, J. (2016). Framework for practitioners 2: The GROWTH model. In C. van Nieuwerburgh (Ed.). *Coaching in professional contexts* (pp. 235–240). London: Sage.

Charteris, J., & Smardon, D. (2014). Dialogic peer coaching as teacher leadership for professional inquiry. *International Journal of Mentoring and Coaching in Education, 3*(2), 108–124.

Cornett, J., & Knight, J. (2008). Research on coaching. In J. Knight (Ed.). *Coaching: Approaches and perspectives* (pp. 192–216). Thousand Oaks: Corwin.

Costa, A. L., & Garmston, R. J. (2003). Cognitive coaching in retrospect: Why it persists. Retrieved from www.thinkingcollaborative.com/wp-content/uploads/2012/08/CC-in-Retrospect-Why-Persists.pdf.

Costa, A. L., & Garmston, R. J. (2015). *Cognitive coaching: Developing self-directed leaders and learners.* London: Rowman & Littlefield.

Danielson, C. (2007). *Enhancing professional practice: A framework for teaching* (2nd ed.). Alexandria: ASCD.

Drago-Severson, E., & Blum-DeStefano, J. (2018). *Leading change together: Developing educator capacity within schools and systems.* Alexandria: ASCD.

Edwards, J. L., & Newton, R. R. (1995). The effects of cognitive coaching on teacher efficacy and empowerment. Paper presented at the Annual Meeting of the American Educational Research Association. San Francisco.

Elliott, E. M., Isaacs, M. L., & Chugani, C. D. (2010). Promoting self-efficacy in early career teachers: A principal's guide for differentiated mentoring and supervision. *Florida Journal of Educational Administration & Policy, 4*(1), 131–146.

Fletcher, S. J. (2012). Coaching: An overview. In S. J. Fletcher & C. A. Mullen (Eds.). *The Sage handbook of mentoring and coaching in education* (pp. 24–40). London: Sage.

Goker, S. D. (2006). Impact of peer coaching on self-efficacy and instructional skills in TEFL teacher education. *System, 34,* 239–254.

Gormley, H., & van Nieuwerburgh, C. (2014). Developing coaching cultures: A review of the literature. *Coaching: an International Journal of Theory, Research and Practice, 7*(2), 90–101.

Hargreaves, A., & Skelton, J. (2012). Politics and systems of coaching and mentoring. In S. J. Fletcher & C. A. Mullen (Eds.). *The Sage handbook of mentoring and coaching in education* (pp. 122–138). London: Sage.

Heikkinen, H. L., Wilkinson, J., Aspfors, J., & Bristol, L. (2018). Understanding mentoring of new teachers: Communicative and strategic practices in Australia and Finland. *Teaching and Teacher Education, 71,* 1–11.

Jack, A. I., Boyatzis, R. E., Khawaja, M. S., Passarelli, A. M., & Leckie, R. L. (2013). Visioning in the brain: An fMRI study of inspirational coaching and mentoring. *Social Neuroscience, 8* (4), 369–384.

Joyce, B., & Showers, B. (1988). *Student achievement through staff development.* New York: Longman.

Kane, T. J., & Staiger, D. O. (2012). *Gathering feedback for teaching: Combining high-quality observations with student surveys and achievement gains.* Research Paper. MET Project. Bill & Melinda Gates Foundation.

Knight, J., & van Nieuwerburgh, C. (2012). Instructional coaching: A focus on practice. *Coaching: an International Journal of Theory, Research and Practice, 5*(2), 100–112.

Kraft, M. A., Blazar, D., & Hogan, D. (2016). The effect of teacher coaching on instruction and achievement: A meta-analysis of the causal evidence. *Review of Educational Research, 88*(4), 547–588.

Lieberman, A., Campbell, C., & Yashkina, A. (2017). *Teacher leadership and learning: Of, by, and for teachers.* Abingdon: Routledge.

Lipton, L., & Wellman, B. M. (2013). *Learning-focused supervision: Developing professional expertise in standards-driven systems.* Charlotte: MiraVia.

Lofthouse, R. (2019). Coaching in education: A professional development process in formation. *Professional Development in Education, 45*(1), 33–45.

Lofthouse, R., & Leat, D. (2013). An activity theory perspective on peer coaching. *International Journal of Mentoring and Coaching in Education, 2*(1), 8–20.

Lofthouse, R., Leat, D., Towler, C., Hallet, E., & Cummings, C. (2010). Improving coaching: Evolution not revolution, research report. National College for Leadership of Schools and Children's services, Newcastle University.

McIntyre, J., & Hobson, A. J. (2016). Supporting beginner teacher identity development: External mentors and the third space. *Research Papers in Education, 31*(2), 133–158.

Munro, C., Barr, M., & van Nieuwerburgh, C. (in press). Creating a whole-school coaching culture for learning. In E. Jackson & A. Berkeley (Eds.). *Keeping your head: Finding and sustaining depth and balance in school leadership.* London: Routledge.

Murray, M. (2001). *Beyond the myths and magic of mentoring: How to facilitate an effective mentoring process.* San Francisco: Jossey-Bass.

Netolicky, D. M. (2016). Coaching for professional growth in one Australian school: "Oil in water". *International Journal of Mentoring and Coaching in Education, 5*(2), 66–86.

Rhodes, C., & Fletcher, S. (2013). Coaching and mentoring for self-efficacious leadership in schools. *International Journal of Mentoring and Coaching in Education, 2*(1), 47.

Showers, J., & Joyce, B. (1996). The evolution of peer coaching. *Educational Leadership, 53*(6), 12–16.

Tonna, M. A., Bjerkholt, E., & Holland, E. (2017). Teacher mentoring and the reflective practitioner approach. *International Journal of Mentoring and Coaching in Education, 6*(3), 210–227.

van Nieuwerburgh, C. (2017). *An introduction to coaching skills: A practical guide* (2nd ed.). London: Sage.

van Nieuwerburgh, C., & Passmore, J. (2012). Creating coaching cultures for learning. In C. van Nieuwerburgh (Ed.). *Coaching in Education: Getting Better Results for Students, Educators, and Parents* (pp. 153–172). London: Karnac.

Whitmore, J. (2009). *Coaching for performance: Growing people, performance and purpose* (4th ed.). London: Nicholas Brealey.

Wiliam, D. (2014). Teacher expertise: Why it matters and how to get more of it. In J. Hallgarten, L. Bamfield, & K. McCarthy (Eds.). *Licensed to create: Ten essays on improving teacher quality* (pp. 27–36). London: Royal Society for the Encouragement of the Arts, Manufactures and Commerce.

Wong, K., & Nicotera, A. (2003). *Enhancing teacher quality: Peer coaching as a professional development strategy: A preliminary synthesis of the literature.* Nashville: Vanderbilt University.

Zepeda, S. J., Parylo, O., & Ilgan, A. (2013). Teacher peer coaching in American and Turkish schools. *International Journal of Mentoring and Coaching in Education, 2*(1), 64–82.

Chapter 6

Self-directed professional learning

In our current world of readily available information, vlogs, blogs, podcasts, massive open online courses, and social media, professional learning is bleeding into people's lives in unexpected ways, and learning is accessible via a changing variety of platforms and modes. Professional learning has moved towards that in which teachers are active learners shaping their own professional growth (Clarke & Hollingsworth, 2002). Increasingly, teachers and school leaders find themselves reaching out to others around the world, or looking for self-directed 'do it yourself' approaches to their own learning. This chapter explores the rapidly growing field of professional learning that is driven by the learner and sometimes sourced in non-traditional ways or ways not readily acknowledged by schools or education bodies. This kind of professional learning is an act of agency. Its increasing popularity with teachers and school leaders suggests: a resistance to cookie cutter PD that assumes a uniformity of professional learners; a seeking of local alternatives to the barrage of experts from afar; and an embracing of professional learning grounded in ownership and autonomy rather than compliance and accountability.

While it might be argued that all learning is self-directed to some extent, learning that concentrates on the autonomy of the learner has been a focus of some education discourse. The words *andragogy*—meaning adult learning (Knowles, 1970; Mezirow, 1985)—and *self-directed learning*—which involves learner-directed activity usually under the guidance of an instructor (Brookfield, 1986; Knowles, 1975)—appeared in research literature in the 1970s and 1980s. Brookfield (1986) positions adult learning as empowering, developing self-worth, and inextricably entwined with all aspects of a person's life, not just their work. Andragogy, proposed as an adult learning alternative to *pedagogy*, is described by Knowles (1970) as "the art and science of helping adults learn" (p. 38), while Jack Mezirow (1985) depicts it as a process that enhances an adult's ability to become increasingly autonomous, responsible, and self-directed in their learning. Andragogy is based on assumptions that adults have an independent self-concept, are intrinsically motivated to learn, can direct their own learning, have life experiences that are a resource for learning, and are influenced by their social roles (Merriam, 2001).

Malcolm Knowles (1975) describes self-directed learning as "a process by which individuals take the initiative, with or without the assistance of others, in diagnosing their learning needs, formulating learning goals, identifying human and material resources for learning, choosing and implementing appropriate learning strategies, and evaluating learning outcomes" (p. 18). Self-directed learning is outlined by Stephen Brookfield (1986) as a process of continual reflection and action that allows adults to "free themselves from externally imposed direction in their learning" in order that they "become proactive, initiating individuals in reshaping their personal, work, political, and recreational lives" (p. 60). *Heutagogy* (Hase & Kenyon, 2000) depicts self-determined learning in which the learner is an initiator and agent of learning. *Self-determination theory* (Ryan & Deci, 2000) posits that the best learning happens in environments that support autonomy and competence, and that excessive control can hinder learning. These authors argue that while learners need to feel like they have control over their learning, they also need to be connected to others; being self-directed doesn't mean being alone. So, self-directed learning assumes that learners have the capacity to own, drive, determine, and propel their own learning. The common thread here is a resistance to control and compliance, and the independence of the learner. While adult education is described as a unique field of practice that could be differentiated from learning in general and from the pedagogy associated with teaching children in schools (Merriam, 2001), students of any age have the capacity to be self-directed and autonomous in their learning; this is not the domain of adult learning alone.

The notion of learning owned and driven by the learner echoes the argument that there is not, nor should there be, a one-size-fits-all approach to professional development. It is also consistent with those who call for teachers to develop autonomy, self-efficacy, and self-reflection as key aspects of professional learning. For example, Helen Timperley (2008) says that teachers need to develop self-regulatory skills that enable them to reflect upon and monitor the effects of any changes to their practice. The act of engaging in reflective practice has been positioned as the catalyst for transformational change in teaching practice (Hayden et al., 2013). Through this lens, professional learning should give participants autonomy in directing their professional learning, be aligned to the needs of participants, and take into account the needs of school and system (Zepeda et al., 2014). Considering voice, choice, agency, and ownership of learning can help professional learning be meaningful and motivating to teachers and school leaders, especially as we tend to be highly critical of ineffective pedagogies or learning that we think fails to meet our needs.

Types of self-directed professional learning

Self-directed learning is about the self-efficacy of the adult learner. It takes a range of forms, which, as time goes on, evolve due to what is possible through technologies and an increasingly connected world. Self-directedness in the context of professional learning for teachers and school leaders can look like practitioner action research, postgraduate study, or use of collaborative and communication technologies such as Twitter and blogging. Action research provides a structured cycle of inquiry for practitioners. It is flexible, challenging, rigorous, and goes beyond the constraints imposed on teachers and schools, allowing autonomy and ownership by the practitioner.

Some scholarship explores forums that bring together connection with others and self-direction. These involve not just teachers from different schools, but teachers from different districts, education systems, and countries, connecting with one another. I argue that these are forms of *connection* rather than *collaboration*. That is, Edcamps, TeachMeets, unconferences, technologies, and social media allow teachers to connect with one another, to find solidarity, and to learn from one another, but not necessarily to collaborate around student learning in the same deep, sustained way that *within school* collaborative practices (such as those discussed in Chapter 4) allow. That being said, educators including myself have found these modes of professional learning to be important in addressing feelings of professional isolation. They expose teachers to practices and thinking from contexts outside their own. They allow teachers and school leaders to reach out to other like-minded educators, but can result in echo chambers of like-minded individuals, rather than the less-enjoyable but potentially more effective collaboration with those in our own schools.

TeachMeets (Garvey, 2017) and Edcamps (Carpenter & Linton, 2016) are examples of professional learning that are both collaborative and self-directed; they are informal, free, voluntary, and participant-driven forms of professional learning (Carpenter & Linton, 2016). Jeffrey Carpenter and Jayme Linton (2016) in their survey of 769 Edcamp participants found that Edcamps were sites of active participation and social construction of knowledge, in which participants were motivated by the opportunity to collaborate with others, to direct their own learning, and to contribute to the learning of others. Their findings support Nathan Bond's (2015) findings that educators prefer participant-driven, teacher-led professional development; and Dorothy McMillan et al.'s (2014) findings that educators feel a strong sense of responsibility for their own professional learning. Carpenter and Linton (2016) conclude that professional learning "can be about more than just learning specific knowledge or skills; it can help teachers see themselves as lifelong learners, continuously adapting in response to students" (p. 104). These examples of how educators are adopting a self-directed approach to professional learning, in their own time and in a variety of places, fuel teachers' perceptions of themselves as professional learners who always work to improve their knowledge and practice.

Below I explore two examples of self-directed professional learning. Firstly, during my PhD research, Twitter emerged as a self-learning platform. Secondly, in my own life I have found various forms of writing to be a kind of self-directed learning that brings together individually-directed learning with collaboration and feedback from others.

Spotlight on research: Twitter for self-directed learning

Participants in my PhD study saw professional learning as a balance between mandated and self-directed learning. Mandated learning was what they had to do, and self-directed learning was what they wanted to do. One teacher explained, "There is some professional learning that you choose to do and there is some professional learning that you don't choose to do but you need to do." School leaders talked about doing some learning for themselves and "a lot of things for compliance."

Professional learning was revealed through my PhD to include 'do it yourself' approaches. Examples shared by my PhD participants included engaging in online platforms and communities to engage with content and individuals. Approaches included professional reading and online collaborative platforms such as Twitter and blogging, which flattened hierarchies and time zones. These were seen as key supports for, and motivators of, learning, for myself and the teacher participants. They allowed us to connect, communicate, and learn from a global community of educators, including teachers, school leaders, researchers, and experts from far and wide. Twitter and blogging were seen as "collaborative global platforms" for connecting with like-minded thinkers and engaging in robust international conversations about education. Engagement with social media alerted us to trends, resources, blog posts, and articles that expanded our knowledge, understanding, and awareness. Teachers felt they "could find support and thinking outside of my immediate environment." One teacher saw Twitter as "an endless supply of professional learning." It is daily, "time effective" "constant PD" that situates them as "part of a worldwide personal learning community" in which hierarchies are collapsed; a description consistent with Fei Gao et al.'s (2012) analyses of 21 2008–2011 studies on microblogging in education.

These emergent findings are also relevant to other studies into Twitter. Educators use Twitter to filter, curate, and share educational content (Holmes et al., 2013), blurring the line between formal and informal learning (Gao et al., 2012). Eric Sheninger (2014), a principal-turned-digital-leadership-consultant who has almost 150,000 Twitter followers at the time of writing, promotes Twitter as a tool for cost-free, autonomous professional learning and collaborative connections. As an "organic and participatory platform," Twitter is both empowering to educators and an antidote to isolation (Carpenter & Krutka, 2015). It can open educators up to voices we would not have encountered in our local education contexts (Barnes & Netolicky, 2018).

Online communities such as Twitter challenge traditional hierarchies and allow members to develop commonalities of identity and the confidence to contribute to global conversations (Stewart, 2015). Twitter provides an individualised experience with rich, interconnected personal learning networks of diverse educators sharing a wide variety of up to date educational material; anytime, anywhere (Carpenter & Krutka, 2015; Gao et al., 2012; Garvey, 2017; Holmes et al., 2013). However, only some teachers are interested in using it for these purposes (Gao et al., 2012).

My PhD study reflected what others have found: that these self-directed and self-determined means can empower educators who seek to be autonomous intellectuals, leaders, and learners, as well as help to overcome isolation and build relationships in a fusion of personal and professional learning.

Spotlight on practice: writing as learning

In my own life, writing has become a form of self-directed professional learning. In my boundary-spanning roles, writing helps me to make sense of my thinking around the intersecting arenas of research, education, teaching, professional learning, and identity. It is a process and product through which I write my way into understanding and test my ideas outside of my own head. The writing itself is self-directed, but it is often through collaborative practices—such as peer review in academic writing or comments on my blog—that my thinking changes and I learn, or am challenged to question my own beliefs and ways of doing things. This experience of learning alone while connected to a community reflects Brookfield's (1986) point that learning within a group brings a rich dimension to self-directed learning. Writing as learning is directed by the individual, but in the world of online publishing, via social media or websites, it is also about being part of a community that writes together.

Writing happens for me on multiple platforms for a range of interconnected purposes. Below I explain how tweeting, blogging, and academic writing all have a place in my own professional learning, and that these can all be both self-directed and collaborative practices.

Since joining Twitter in 2009, I have developed my use of microblogging as one way to write, to engage with others, and thereby to learn. Back then, tweets were limited to 140 characters each and, for a naturally verbose person like me, were an exercise in concision. I was forced through tweeting to distil my thinking down into pithy bites. Being restricted by the writing platform to aphoristically express an idea or viewpoint in a nutshell forced me to crystallise my thinking down into its essence, without agonising over it. As someone who tends to over-write, microblogging forces me to streamline my thoughts and use fewer words. Now that a tweet can run to 250 characters I don't have to think so hard about whittling down my thoughts.

Tweeting can also be a kind of speed writing and speed thinking, especially in an education Twitter chat. During 2015, 2016, and 2017, I co-moderated an education Twitter chat called #EduCoachOC. It was a one-hour monthly online chat about coaching in education, at a time friendly for those in Oceania. The chat ran was preceded by a blog post and a series of pre-scheduled questions to run over the hour. It would attract participants from Australia, New Zealand, the USA, Canada, the UAE, Saudi Arabia, Taiwan, China, and Ghana. Being in this chat meant participating in a firehose of tweets about coaching in education, usually directed around a sub-topic of coaching. Twitter chats like this can provide staff-room-like conversations that bring people from different schools and education systems together around topics of shared interest. Participants are exposed to thinking and practice from a range of contexts.

In 2014, I began my personal blog, theeduflaneuse.com. Initially, the blog was intended for a short term purpose: to record my experiences of a professional learning fellowship to New York. In this way it was simultaneously a site for learning and an accountability mechanism. It was a multimodal and immediate way to record my reflections each day, and to report back to my school the fruits of their investment in my learning. After the fellowship ended, however, I found that blogging itself was a potentially useful vehicle for learning. I didn't stop. I shared thoughts and experiences around education, coaching, leadership, and parenting.

I additionally used blogging as a way to reflect on my PhD candidature. It turns out that for PhD candidates, blogging can reduce isolation, build relationships, form community, and increase the likelihood of completing the doctorate (Brabazon, 2018). In their survey of 193 PhD candidates who also wrote blogs, Inger Mewburn and Pat Thomson (2018) found that PhD students blog for four main reasons: creating a scholarly persona, slow thinking, pleasure seeking, and knowledge sharing. Like me, other PhD candidates blog in order to 'freeze' and make visible their thinking. Mewburn and Thomson's (2018) finding—that blogging is a site for creating a sense of belonging via correspondence with a niche readership community—resonates with my own experience.

Over the last few years my blogging schedule has looked different. Sometimes my blog writing has been ad hoc, sometimes I have blogged fortnightly, and sometimes I have blogged weekly. In 2018 I decided to slow down my blog writing so that I could concentrate my writing energy into editing *Flip the System Australia*, and into proposing and beginning this book. By the end of 2018, my blog had been viewed over 100,000 times in over 150 countries and had over 200 individual blog posts. This is not impressive in blogging terms, but shows that I have connected with people as a result of my blog writing, their reading, and our subsequent online, face to face, and voice to voice conversations. Blogging continues to be a form of self-directed learning, a way to clarify my thinking, test it with a global audience, contribute to international education discourses, and communicate research findings.

Academic writing has also been a powerful self-directed learning experience for me. It began with my PhD, during which I self-directed, with the guidance of my supervisors, a sustained research study. The PhD necessitated an ongoing and sometimes uncomfortable process of reading relevant literatures, planning next milestones, writing and rewriting, thinking and rethinking. It was a sustained and ongoing experience of being a student who was both autonomous and mentored. It was an exercise in persistence, humility, and resilience. Getting feedback from my supervisors on my writing brought a collaborative feedback dimension to the often isolated work and learning of the PhD.

Other forms of academic writing such as abstracts, journal articles, book chapters, and conference papers require different ways of writing, working, thinking, and learning. Each of these comes with checks and balances in the form of editors and reviewers who evaluate and provide feedback. Blind peer review is not always pleasant, but it is a vehicle for learning and improving. While at some stages of writing this book, I missed the feedback that other forms of writing provide, it was helpful and honest feedback from pre-publication readers that helped to strengthen it. The capacity to give and receive honest but critical feedback has spilled over into my work life, as I attempt to build a culture of learning and feedback that is constructive but not always easy to share or to hear.

Public, collaborative writing can be a vehicle for rewarding and transformational learning. Naomi Barnes and I have written about our own collaboration that began via Twitter, moved on to our blogs, and then ended up in journal articles and book chapters (Barnes & Netolicky, 2018; Netolicky & Barnes, 2019). In our book chapter on how we have used technologies to write together (Netolicky & Barnes, 2019), we say that "our differences have allowed us to write in ways that we would be unable to write alone" (p. 177) and that "online is a place we think out loud, and in doing so, we have become connected with individuals, which in turn become webbed networks of scholars and educators" (p. 167). I have been shaped and re-formed by my writerly collaborations (Barnes & Netolicky, 2018). Writing for different purposes and audiences has been a self-directed, but simultaneously connected, learning experience for me.

Key takeaways

- Some learning for teachers and school leaders is mandated and must be completed for regulatory or compliance reasons.
- Self-directed learning is a process of continual reflection and action in which learners are proactive, initiating individuals who reshape their work and lives. It assumes that learners have the capacity to own, drive, determine, and propel their own learning.
- Andragogy is a term used to describe the pedagogy of adult learning, focused on self-directedness. However, any learner has the capacity to be self-directed, regardless of age.
- Heutagogy is a word used to refer to self-determined learning, under-pinned by a belief in learners as initiators and agents of their own learning.
- Educators are increasingly turning to 'do it yourself' professional learning, including postgraduate study, writing, TeachMeets, Edcamps, and online platforms such as Twitter and blogging.
- Professional networks or events can offer connection but not necessarily learning.
- Self-directed learning can be an act of agency.

References

Barnes, N., & Netolicky, D. M. (2018). Cutting apart together: A diffracted spatial history of an online scholarly relationship. *International Journal of Qualitative Studies in Education, 32*(4), 1–14.

Bond, N. (2015). Teacher leaders and professional developers. In N. Bond (Ed.). *Perspectives on teacher leadership: Their roles, influence, and impact* (pp. 57–69). New York: Routledge.

Brabazon, T. (2018). The deficit doctorate: Multimodal solutions to enable differentiated learning. *International Journal of Social Sciences & Educational Studies, 4*(5), 52–70.

Brookfield, S. D. (1986). *Understanding and facilitating adult learning: A comprehensive analysis of principles and effective practices.* Buckingham: Open University Press.

Carpenter, J. P., & Krutka, D. G. (2015). Engagement through microblogging: Educator professional development via Twitter. *Professional Development in Education, 41*(4), 702–728.

Carpenter, J. P., & Linton, J. N. (2016). Edcamp unconferences: Educators' perspectives on an untraditional professional learning experience. *Teaching and Teacher Education, 57*, 97–108.

Clarke, D., & Hollingsworth, H. (2002). Elaborating a model of teacher professional growth. *Teaching and Teacher Education, 18*(8), 947–967.

Gao, F., Luo, T., & Zhang, K. (2012). Tweeting for learning: A critical analysis of research on microblogging in education published in 2008–2011. *British Journal of Educational Technology, 43*(5), 783–801.

Garvey, P. (2017). *Talk for teaching: Completely rethinking professional development in schools.* Melton: John Catt.

Hase, S., & Kenyon, C. (2000). *From andragogy to heutagogy.* Melbourne: Ulti-BASE In-Site.

Hayden, H. E., Moore-Russo, D., & Marino, M. R. (2013). One teacher's reflective journey and the evolution of a lesson: Systematic reflection as a catalyst for adaptive expertise. *Reflective Practice, 14*(1), 144–156.

Holmes, K., Preston, G., Shaw, K., & Buchanan, R. (2013). 'Follow' me: Networked professional learning for teachers. *Australian Journal of Teacher Education, 38*(12), 55–65.

Knowles, M. S. (1970). *The modern practice of adult education: From pedagogy to andragogy.* Oxford: Association Press.

Knowles, M. S. (1975). *Self-directed learning: A guide for learners and teachers.* New York: Association Press.

McMillan, D. J., McConnell, B., & O'Sullivan, H. (2014). Continuing professional development, why bother? Perceptions and motivations of teachers in Ireland. *Professional Development in Education, 42*(1), 150–167.

Merriam, S. B. (2001). Andragogy and self-directed learning: Pillars of adult learning theory. *New Directions for Adult and Continuing Education, 89,* 3–14.

Mewburn, I., & Thomson, P. (2018). Towards an academic self?: Blogging during the doctorate. In D. Lupton, I. Mewburn, & P. Thomson (Eds.). *The digital academic: Critical perspectives on digital technologies in higher education* (pp. 20–35). Abingdon: Routledge.

Mezirow, J. (1985). Concept and action in adult education. *Adult Education Quarterly, 35*(3), 142–151.

Netolicky, D. M., & Barnes, N. (2019). Scholarship of the cyborg: Productivities and undercurrents. In A. Baroutsis, S. Riddle, & P. Thomson (Eds.). *Education research and the media: Challenges and possibilities* (pp. 165–179). Abingdon: Routledge.

Ryan, R. M., & Deci, E. L. (2000). Self-determination theory and the facilitation of intrinsic motivation, social development, and well-being. *American Psychologist, 55*(1), 68–78.

Sheninger, E. (2014). *Digital leadership: Changing paradigms for changing times.* Moorabin: Hawker Brownlow Education.

Stewart, B. (2015). Open to influence: What counts as academic influence in scholarly networked Twitter participation. *Learning, Media and Technology, 40*(3), 287–309.

Timperley, H. (2008). *Teacher professional learning and development: Educational practices series 18.* Brussels: International Academy of Education, International Bureau of Education & UNESCO.

Zepeda, S. J., Parylo, O., & Bengtson, E. (2014). Analysing principal professional development practices through the lens of adult learning theory. *Professional Development in Education, 40*(2), 295–315.

Chapter 7

The role of professional standards in professional learning

All professions work towards consensus about what it means to be a member of that profession (Darling-Hammond et al., 2009) and a set of professional standards can add legitimacy and status to a profession. In 2005, Helen Wildy and Coral Pepper wrote that *standards* have been one of the most dominant metaphors in education in the last decade. More than a decade has passed since then, and standards continue to be a prominent part of education discourse, policy, and practice.

Teacher standards are now embedded in education systems, and have a direct impact on the ways in which teaching is conceptualised and professional learning is designed, advertised, and undertaken. Professional learning is often tied to national standards. There is the question, however, of whether professional standards are a help or hindrance to the professional learning and capacity building of the teaching profession. Standards as mechanisms of control (Sachs, 2003) have emerged from the snowballing teacher quality agenda, described in this book's Introduction. They can be seen as an attempt to standardise, regulate, and control the teaching profession. For example, enhancing teacher quality is articulated as the overarching goal of the Australia's Professional Standards for Teachers (Clinton et al., 2015). Teacher standards are often policy apparatuses intended to assess and improve teacher quality (Clinton et al., 2015). They influence professional learning worldwide, and frame discussions and expectations around what it means to be a teacher.

Professional standards have potential advantages for teaching, leading, and professional learning. Some argue that teachers and school leaders can benefit from a common 'map' (Fleming & Kleinhenz, 2007) that provides a clear definition of practice, transparent standards, evidence to be gathered, and a language for meaningful professional discourse. Standards can be rallying points for useful professional conversations that set aspirations for goal setting and growth, providing the *what* to talk about (Lipton & Wellman, 2012), as well as common, clear understandings about what is regarded as good practice (McKay, 2013). They can be a vehicle for deprivatising teacher practice (Garmston & Wellman, 2013) through the opening up of classrooms to observation and professional dialogue. They can provide provocation for teachers to think about their work and identity in meaningful ways (Sachs, 2003).

Mihaly Csikszentmihalyi et al. (2011) found that clear standards for what constitutes desirable performance can support 'good work.' They argue that standards should be endorsed and enforced by the professional community, internalised in the self-image of practitioners, and that people need to have time and opportunity to formally and deeply reflect on standards if they are to be meaningful. They warn, however, that external economic, political, and social forces should not contradict professional standards.

The use of standards as a framework for teacher learning, and pressure for teachers to undertake professional learning linked to professional standards, can intensify teacher workload (Sachs, 2003). Standards-based professional learning should be seen as an integral part of teachers' work with time allocated for it to occur. So, well-articulated and research-supported standards can provide common language and reference points for talking about teaching, coaching, and leading. However, these are ideally owned and overseen by the profession (Sachs, 2003), not by external or government forces seeking to control the profession.

This chapter discusses the role and purpose of teacher standards in teacher reflection, coaching, and evaluation. It provides an overview of standards used in England, the USA, and Australia, as well as independent standards frameworks, in order to understand the landscape of professional standards, the ways in which they are being deployed around the world, and their role in professional learning.

National professional standards

English national standards for teachers

In England, a national set of teaching standards (Department of Education England, 2011) outlines the minimum level of practice expected of teachers. The standards address both teaching practice (in Part One) and teacher conduct (in Part Two). The teaching practices expected of teachers are described as encompassing the following eight areas.

- Setting high expectations which inspire, motivate and challenge pupils.
- Promoting good progress and outcomes by pupils.
- Demonstrating good subject and curriculum knowledge.
- Planning and teaching well-structured lessons.
- Adapting teaching to respond to the strengths and needs of all pupils.
- Making accurate and productive use of assessment.
- Managing behaviour effectively to ensure a good and safe learning environment.
- Fulfilling wider professional responsibilities.

These are used to assess the suitability and performance of all teachers, including trainee teachers, newly qualified teachers, and experienced teachers.

Part Two of the standards, which describes the values, attitudes, ethics, and behaviour expected of teachers, is applied by the National College for Teaching and Leadership when hearing cases of personal or professional misconduct. In this way the standards act as a measure and a punitive tool.

USA national standards for teachers

In the USA, the National Board of Professional Teaching Standards, which was founded in 1987, published their set of standards in 1989, and updated these in 2016 (NBPTS, 2016). The standards are based around five core propositions, as follows.

- Teachers are committed to students and their learning.
- Teachers know the subjects they teach and how to teach those subjects to students.
- Teachers are responsible for managing and monitoring student learning.
- Teachers think systematically about their practice and learn from experience.
- Teachers are members of learning communities.

These standards have become widespread, incorporated into teacher education, accreditation, and professional learning (Darling-Hammond et al., 2009).

Australian national standards for teachers

The Australian Professional Standards for Teachers were released in 2011 by AITSL, providing teachers with a national set of standards outlining what teachers "should know and be able to do." The TEMAG report (Craven et al., 2014) recommended a strengthened national quality assurance process for initial teacher accreditation, including evidence that all graduate teachers meet the graduate level of the professional standards.

The Australian Professional Standards for Teachers are split into three domains and seven standards, as follows.

- Professional knowledge.

  - Know students and how they learn.
  - Know the content and how to teach it.

- Professional practice.

  - Plan for and implement effective teaching and learning.
  - Create and maintain supportive and safe learning environments.
  - Assess, provide feedback and report on student learning.

- Professional engagement.

  - Engage in professional learning.
  - Engage professionally with colleagues, parents/carers and the community.

The Australian standards are organised into linear career progression beginning at *graduate* and continuing to *proficient, highly accomplished*, and *lead*. These stages are intended to reflect the processes through which teachers pass during their careers. Graduate teachers are accredited, proficient teachers gain and maintain teacher registration, and when teachers want to demonstrate excellence, in many Australian states they can apply to be recognised as a highly accomplished or lead teacher, and sometimes remunerated with a higher salary. The assumption of a linear progression, however, does not take into account the variation in teachers at different times in their careers, such as those early career teachers who collaborate and lead initiatives.

The Australian standards were developed and implemented in consultation with educators (Clinton et al., 2015) but are now attached to teacher registration, evaluation, performance metrics, and professional learning. Currently, teacher registration is managed at state and territory level by local teacher regulatory authorities. The argument for compulsory teacher registration is that it contributes to the professionalisation of the teaching workforce as teachers are expected to meet a certain standard of education, experience, and personal characteristics to become part of, and maintain their membership of, the teaching profession (AITSL, 2018). In 2018, a national review of Australian teacher registration (AITSL, 2018) found that there is inconsistency between jurisdictions in the way that teacher registration requirements are interpreted and administered, and that the lack of consistency across the country hinders workforce mobility and erodes the effectiveness and application of the professional standards.

In Australia a mandated minimum 20 hours per year of professional learning is required by full-time teachers. Evidence of this learning, mapped to the professional standards, is needed to support a teacher's accreditation as a member of the profession. In some states, some of this professional learning is required to be provided by an approved body. The aim in Australia is that teachers view professional registration as an opportunity for professional growth and a hallmark of being a professional; and that professional learning is based on need, has strong connections with the roles and expectations of teachers, and leads to a change in the knowledge, behaviours, and actions of teachers (AITSL, 2018). Teachers, however, view the registration requirements for professional learning as compliance-focused, with limited support for connecting learning to practice (AITSL, 2018). There seems a gap between the intentions of the standards, their use, and teachers' experiences of them.

The Danielson Framework for Teaching

As well as national standards, there are teaching standards such as those outlined in Robert Marzano's Causal Teacher Evaluation Model (Marzano, 2007), the Quality Teaching Framework (Bowe & Gore, 2017) and Charlotte Danielson's Framework for Teaching (Danielson, 2008). Marzano's model claims that using instructional strategies of the model improves student achievement and helps teachers develop themselves professionally (Marzano et al., 2012). The Quality Teaching Framework is intended to provide a broad knowledge base around teaching and facilitate specificity of lesson analysis and rich professional conversations that improve student learning and narrow equity gaps (Bowe & Gore, 2017). Here I describe the Framework for Teaching because it was the framework used in the coaching model I implemented in my school, and studied for my PhD, and also because it has been identified as a research-based set of standards.

Danielson's Framework—explained in the most detail in *Enhancing Professional Practice: A Framework for Teaching* (Danielson, 2008)—provides a map of what excellence in teaching might look like, with a set of shared, explicit descriptors. Grounded in research, it is a thorough, multi-layered definition of good teaching that identifies a comprehensive range of teacher responsibilities. The Framework clusters its 22 components of teaching into four domains of teacher responsibility, as follows.

- Domain 1: Planning and Preparation.
- Domain 2: The Classroom Environment.
- Domain 3: Instruction.
- Domain 4: Professional Responsibilities.

While these components are separated for the purpose of the Framework, they are acknowledged as interrelated parts of a complex holistic endeavour. The components are intended to be applicable to diverse settings and independent of any particular teaching methodology. In action, the Framework is more web-like than grid-like. This is reflected in the choice of cover artwork for *The Framework for Teaching Evaluation Instrument* (Danielson, 2013) which shows the four domains as an intersecting Venn diagram.

The Danielson Framework for Teaching was studied as part of the Measures of Effective Teaching (MET) project, a three-year research project launched by the Bill and Melinda Gates Foundation in 2009 (Kane & Staiger, 2012). The MET study analysed 23,000 lessons of 3,000 teacher volunteers in six USA urban school districts in order to investigate how teacher practice affects student achievement. It found that the Framework:

- was positively associated with student achievement gains;
- focused observers' attention on specific aspects of teaching practice;
- established common evidentiary standards for each level of practice; and
- created a common vocabulary for pursuing a shared vision of effective instruction.

The MET project also concluded that, when implementing an instrument for teacher evaluation (or, in my school's case, reflection and growth):

- clear standards and multiple observations are required when evaluating a teacher's practice;
- evaluation systems should include multiple measures;
- combining observation scores with evidence of student achievement gains and student feedback improved predictive power and reliability, and identified teachers with larger gains on state tests; and
- the true promise of classroom observations is the potential to identify strengths and address specific weaknesses in teachers' practice.

In Dylan Wiliam's (2016) book, *Leadership for teacher learning*, he spends seven pages (pp. 45–51) outlining the research findings around the Danielson

Framework. While he cautions that the Framework is limited, especially in its ability to differentiate variation among teachers, he describes it as "rigorously researched" (p. 45) and "the best we can do in relating student progress to classroom observations" (p. 51). Wiliam points out that it has been shown that students taught by teachers who are rated highly on the Framework make more progress. In fact, students taught by a teacher rated as 'distinguished' make almost 30% more progress than those rated as 'unsatisfactory.' For my school, during our use of the Danielson Framework—from 2012–2016—our focus was on each teacher looking at low inference lesson data at a particular moment in time. They interrogated where the evidence placed that data against Danielson's Framework, by themselves, or as calibrated with a coach or manager.

One thing that resonated with me with the Framework for Teaching was Charlotte Danielson's insistence that it is a tool for conversation, reflection, and improvement, not one for evaluation. She argues that teachers, from veterans to novices, should strive to improve, not because they aren't good enough, but because they can always be better in their complex work (Danielson, 2007).

When I met with Charlotte Danielson in Princeton in October of 2014, she told me that "the opposite of judgement is not 'do nothing'." That is, the use of a standards framework does not mean there is no judgement at all about a teacher's teaching, but rather that the judgement is not punitive or evaluative in nature. It is focused on growth and improvement, for the benefit of the students. By interrogating classroom evidence against a framework, a teacher engages in judgement of their own practice. A colleague or manager might collaborate around those observations and reflections, operating as a calibrator of the teacher's thinking against the standards. The standards provide an objective frame for observation, reflection, conversation, and consequent action.

A word of warning on professional standards

Explicit, shared professional standards can provide a map of what good teaching looks like, commonality of language, and a framework for rich professional conversations around practice. At first glance, lists of professional standards for teachers provide an unsurprising overview of teachers' work. They make a lot of sense. In practice, however, the nitty gritty of what each standard looks like when done well, is much less clear.

The use of professional standards needs careful consideration. They have been criticised for ignoring the complex, critical, and contextualised nature of teaching, aiming instead to create the illusion of certainty and promoting an uncritical and compliant profession. They can be an unhelpful means of control and governance. They value decontextualised traits and behaviours that construct a particular version of 'what works' (Niesche & Thomson, 2017).

Glenn Savage and Bob Lingard (2018) point out that the purpose of standards is "to seek to standardise and ostensibly improve practice in line with common expectations of practice" (p.78). They warn that such processes of standardisation are informed by a narrowing body of evidence, influence, and expertise. In particular, the range of research used to construct concepts like 'student achievement,' 'teacher quality,' and 'effectiveness' is limited, with the OECD playing a particularly powerful role in informing how these are framed for the profession.

Additionally, teacher classroom practice is teachers' arena of greatest anxiety, insecurity, and vulnerability (Goodson, 1991) and teachers are often fearful of initiatives that open the classroom door in order to look at teachers' classroom practice (Louis, 2006). Rather than placing teacher attention on the most exposed and vulnerable aspect of their work, Ivor Goodson (1991) advocates listening to teachers, and thereby valuing and capturing their voices about life and work. So while reflecting on standards might help teachers to grow, it places teachers in a heightened state of vulnerability.

To sum up, frameworks that map teaching standards may provide a valuable starting point for conversations about teaching practice, but unquestioningly adhering to them is not a recipe for improving teaching. They can provide a basis for professional reflection and development, but not (as they are used in some places) as a scorecard for assessing teacher performance. Standards are best used as catalysts for reflection rather than models of growth in themselves. A formative focus on continuous improvement is an appropriate lens for the use of teaching standards and frameworks if our aim is to improve the learning of our students through professional learning that transforms the teaching of our teachers. Rather than being solutions to developing quality teaching, mapping frameworks are tools that can be added to a school or system's arsenal of resources to help build clear, shared understandings of good teaching, incite rich professional conversations around practice, and encourage individual teachers to reflect on and adjust their teaching.

Spotlight on research: the Danielson Framework for Teaching

During the coaching intervention at my school, we used the Framework for Teaching in the following ways.

- Coaches and managers were trained by a Danielson consultant in generating lesson data and using the Framework in professional conversations.
- Teachers completed an annual online self-reflection against the Framework, in order to surface reflections about their teaching, help them set goals, and guide their thinking as they planned for the year ahead.
- During coaching conversations, coaches helped teachers to consider their lesson data against the Framework, looking closely at the descriptors and facilitating reflection against the rubrics.
- The Danielson Framework sat alongside the Australian National Professional Standards for Teachers as a tool for deepening reflection and conversation about practice, allowing teachers to more specifically envisage, articulate, and enact excellence in teaching practice. It provided more specificity than the national standards.

While the Danielson Framework for Teaching was an important element of the coaching intervention, it was implemented alongside an observation and coaching model that helped to draw out teachers' reflections; the lesson data, conversation, and development of a collaborative professional learning culture were vital parts of the application of the Framework. The coaching intervention sat alongside other school-based processes such as formal probation, evaluation, and performance management; and was in addition to other professional learning opportunities.

It became clear during my PhD study that developing their understanding of the Danielson Framework for Teaching impacted teacher participants' classroom practice and helped them to apply more specificity in reflections about teaching and in professional goal setting. Teachers' knowledge of the 'distinguished' teaching descriptors from the Framework shaped their classroom practice; they were conscious of these before, during, and after teaching. Once familiar with the Framework, teachers would make classroom decisions based on aiming for those 'distinguished' descriptors, and later discuss those conscious decisions during coaching conversations. Teacher participants remarked that they brought their mental recollection of the Framework into their lessons, adjusting teaching according to their shared knowledge of what excellent teaching could look like.

The Danielson Framework was seen by participants of this study as having the potential to facilitate a common language about teaching in a school, and encourage precise teacher reflection on practice. As one teacher noted, the Framework shows a "continuum of practice," offering something objective for any teacher "to measure against," regardless of discipline or year level. Across the school, teachers from diverse areas were able to understand these explicit standards as well as be "able to clearly articulate what quality teaching might look like using a common language and even having the rubrics to break it down."

Moments of professional growth for me and for the teachers involved in the coaching intervention tended to be those in which we felt dissonance, but were supported. I noted that I "didn't focus on the things I was really happy with" but "on the things I wanted to improve." I realised that this choice led to dis-comfort rather than enjoyment. I observed that "where I was enjoying myself most was in chatting with colleagues about things that interested me, but that wasn't necessarily where I was learning." The learning happened in honest reflection against the Danielson Framework for Teaching and subsequent strat-egies to improve teaching practice. One teacher noted that the Framework had resulted in them "raising my standards in alignment with it" and "really reflect-ing on what I do." Teachers found themselves mentally rating their classroom practice against the teaching rubric and using it for professional reflection, resulting in shifts in practice. "I've definitely changed, even just little aspects of lessons and planning and things like that. Just from an awareness of that rubric and that framework."

This PhD study revealed that cognitive coaching and the Danielson Frame-work for Teaching can be congruent tools for positive teacher growth, requiring a slow bottom up approach to change, an organisational culture of trust, and coaching relationships free from judgement or power inequity. Maps of what teacher quality looks like, such as the Danielson Framework for Teaching, can be utilised to develop a common understanding of what makes good practice and as the basis for professional conversation. The coaching intervention's use of the Danielson Framework in conjunction with cognitive coaching reflects a focus on growth and building efficacy, rather than evaluation, contrived collegiality, and compliance.

Despite study participants' generally positive responses to the Framework for Teaching, one middle leader questioned the Framework's compartmentalisation and atomisation of teaching into parts. This person was wary of the Framework's potential to fracture teachers' discussion of their teaching, disregarding the complex and holistic nature of teaching. This leader was "concerned about atomising bits [of teaching] … the process then becomes decontextualised and … we have lost the big picture because we have focused on these little bits." This caution was reflected by another leader's comment that "one size does not fit all" and that "different things apply to different people." For example, using the Danielson Framework for Teaching with a "reductionist approach" that might be more useful, even "fantastic," for younger teachers, but not for very experienced teachers.

Spotlight on practice: Australian professional standards for goal setting, reflection, and development

In recent years, my school, like others around Australia, has been working towards embedding and engaging with our national professional standards. In our case, these are the AITSL professional standards for teachers and principals. From 2017, we moved away from using the Danielson Framework for Teaching, not because we considered the Australian standards better, but because they are our national standards. They outline expectations for Australian teachers, and are transferrable across sectors and districts. They encapsulate the language of practice with which Australian teachers are expected to be familiar, and are national mechanisms of probation, registration, and evaluation.

Our teachers were keen to use the national language of professional practice and the Australian standards are intended to provide a common language of practice for teachers across Australia. They point teachers in the direction of what they should know and be able to do, and the AITSL website provides exemplars of practice, but the standards themselves remain fairly vague. So, one the one hand it is great that around the vast nation of Australia, teachers have a shared language of what our work entails, but the standards themselves are open to a wide array of interpretations and applications.

Despite the challenges, my school has embedded the national standards in the following ways.

- Embedding the language of the standards in our documentation of induction, probation, professional development, and professional learning application forms.
- Using the teacher and principal professional standards as the basis for annual teacher and leader self-reflection and goal setting.

- Using the teacher professional standards as a framework for classroom observations and evaluative comments by line managers.
- Using the highly accomplished teacher professional standards as the basis for promotional teaching allowances.
- Using the lead teacher professional standards as the basis for staff applications for mentoring and action research projects.

The national professional standards have been used in this way as a tool for goal setting, reflection, and professional development, as well as on occasion for evaluation or appraisal. In the last couple of years, we have also used them as a strategic tool, selecting one to three standards each year that align with the school's strategic priorities, in order to align teachers' work and reflection with the whole school direction.

Key takeaways

- Professional standards can be seen as a policy mechanism intended to assess and improve teacher quality.
- Professional standards influence professional learning worldwide, and frame discussions and expectations around what it means to be a teacher.
- Around the world, professional standards for teachers are used in teacher education, accreditation or registration, professional learning, performance evaluation, and to assess cases of misconduct.
- Well-articulated and research-supported professional standards can provide a common map of teaching and a common language of practice, useful for professional conversation.
- Ideally, professional standards are owned and used by the profession, not by external forces seeking to control the profession. For professional learning, professional standards should be a formative tool for conversation, reflection, and continuous improvement, not one for evaluation.

References

Australian Institute for Teaching and School Leadership (AITSL). (2018). *One teaching profession: Teacher registration in Australia.*

Bowe, J., & Gore, J. (2017). Reassembling teacher professional development: The case for quality teaching rounds. *Teachers and Teaching, 23*(3), 352–366.

Clinton, J., Dinham, S., Savage, G., Aston, R., Dabrowski, A., Gullickson, A., Calnin, G., & Arbour, G. (2015). *Evaluation of the Australian professional standards for teachers: Final report.* Melbourne: Centre for Program Evaluation, The University of Melbourne.

Craven, G., Beswick, K., Fleming, J., Fletcher, T., Green, M., Jensen, B., Leinonen, E., & Ricjards, F. (2014). *Action now: Classroom ready teachers.* Canberra: Teacher Education Ministerial Advisory Group.

Csikszentmihalyi, M., Damon, W., & Gardner, H. (2011). *The goodwork project: An overview.* Cambridge, MA: The GoodWork Project.

Danielson, C. (2007). *Enhancing professional practice: A framework for teaching* (2nd ed.). Alexandria: ASCD.

Danielson, C. (2008). *The handbook for enhancing professional practice: Using the framework for teaching in your school.* Alexandria: ASCD.

Danielson, C. (2013). *The Framework for teaching evaluation instrument: 2013 edition.* Princeton: The Danielson Group.

Darling-Hammond, L., Wei, R. C., Andree, A., Richardson, N., & Orphanos, S. (2009). *Professional learning in the learning profession.* Washington: National Staff Development Council.

Department of Education England. (2011). *Teachers' standards: Guidance for school leaders, school staff and governing bodies.* Manchester.

Fleming, J., & Kleinhenz, E. (2007). *Towards a moving school: Developing a professional learning and performance culture.* Camberwell: Australian Council for Education Research.

Garmston, R. J., & Wellman, B. (2013). *Adaptive schools: A sourcebook for developing collaborative groups* (2nd ed.). Lanham: Rowman & Littlefield.

Goodson, I. F. (1991). Teachers' lives and educational research. In I. F. Goodson & R. Walker (Eds.). *Biography, identity and schooling: Episodes in educational research* (pp. 137–149). London: Falmer.

Kane, T. J., & Staiger, D. O. (2012). *Gathering feedback for teaching: Combining high-quality observations with student surveys and achievement gains.* MET Research Paper, Bill and Melinda Gates Foundation.

Lipton, L., & Wellman, B. M. (2012). *Got data? Now what?: Creating and leading cultures of inquiry.* Bloomington: Solution Tree.

Louis, K. S. (2006). *Organising for school change: Contexts of learning.* Abingdon: Routledge.

Marzano, R. J. (2007). *The art and science of teaching: A comprehensive framework for effective instruction.* Alexandria: ASCD.

Marzano, R. J., Toth, M., & Schooling, P. (2012). *Examining the role of teacher evaluation in student achievement: Contemporary research base for the Marzano Causal Teacher Evaluation Model.* Blairsville: Learning Science Marzano Centre.

McKay, C. B. (2013). *You don't have to be bad to get better: A leader's guide to improving teacher quality.* Thousand Oaks: Corwin.

National Board for Professional Teaching Standards (NBPTS). (2016). *What teachers should know and be able to do.* Arlington: National Board for Professional Teaching Standards.

Niesche, R., & Thomson, P. (2017). Freedom to what ends? School autonomy in neoliberal times. In D. Waite & I. Bogotch (Eds.). *The Wiley international handbook of educational leadership* (pp. 193–206). Hoboken: Wiley.

Sachs, J. (2003). Teacher professional standards: Controlling or developing teaching? *Teachers and Teaching, 9*(2), 175–186.

Savage, G. C., & Lingard, B. (2018). Changing modes of governance in Australian teacher education policy. In N. Hobbel & B. L. Bales (Eds.). *Navigating the common good in teacher education policy: Critical and international perspectives* (pp. 74–90). New York: Routledge.

Wildy, H., & Pepper, C. (2005). Using narratives to develop standards for leaders: Applying an innovative approach in Western Australia. *Education Research and Perspectives, 32*(2), 122–141.

Wiliam, D. (2016). *Leadership for teacher learning: Creating a culture where all teachers improve so that all students succeed.* Moorabbin: Hawker Brownlow Education.

Chapter 8

Leadership for professional learning

This chapter draws on research literature on school change and leadership to outline the school-based conditions required for effective leadership of trans- formational professional learning. I argue that: leadership of professional learning means considering leadership throughout schools, not just those at the top; schools and systems need to build cultures of trust; the role of research and data needs to be cautiously considered; and leaders can and should be willing to resist policies that encourage competition and visible performance over productive collaboration and authentic growth.

The work of educational leaders is not just technical or administrative; it includes the education of educators as well as students, and also the education of administrators, policymakers, and legislators (Wilkinson & Kemmis, 2015). Lead- ers have a major influence on workplace learning and culture (Eraut, 2012). They develop and implement processes, protocols, norms, expectations, and relationships that support professional learning and growth. They influence and facilitate school culture, but leadership of schools and of professional learning is more than culture. Professional learning that enables teacher agency—teachers' active contribution to shaping their work and its conditions—is necessary in order to transform beliefs and practices. Effective school leadership that facilitates teacher agency is a matter of culture, structure, and relationships, operating as a dynamic, complex interrelated ecology (Duignan, 2012; Grootenboer, 2018).

Leading professional learning is made complex by the range of needs of staff who are at different stages of their career. New graduate teachers don't know what they don't know, but are often eager for new learning. Veteran teachers may feel that they have seen it all before in the cycle of endless school reform, and have little willingness for embracing what the school or system promotes as its latest priority. Many teachers at any career stage may feel like they wish all the administration, co- curricular responsibilities, extra duties, and mandated professional learning would just stop, so they can get on with their core business of teaching.

There is an internet meme that conveys a conversation between a CFO and a CEO. It goes as follows.

CFO: What happens if we train them, and they leave?
CEO: What happens if we don't, and they stay?

This reflects the kind of cost-benefit analysis school leaders undertake when con- sidering investing in staff professional learning. The time that professional learning takes is a consideration of school leaders. Teachers missing lessons for their own learning impacts on student learning, and relief lessons cost money, so it's important that any professional learning that happens during lesson time has a real and relevant benefit. The answer might seem to be that teachers use holidays, weekends, and evenings for professional learning, but this can have a teacher wellbeing cost. Professional learning is also a significant financial cost for schools. Schools and their leaders have to make careful decisions not only around how they allocate professional learning budgets, time, and resourcing; but also on the potential impacts of the scheduling of professional learning on students and staff. There are real benefits to investing in professional learning, and also ways to build school cultures in which staff feel valued, supported, and that they belong.

Much leadership scholarship assumes that visionary leadership—usually by the charismatic CEO or principal figure—is a powerful, indispensable force for good (Tourish, 2013). Leaders at the top of organisations are often still promoted as inspirational, often masculine, hero figures (Netolicky, 2018a, 2018b). Research on leadership tends to focus on the positive, the normative, and the optimistic, rather than that which is weak, absent, or damaging (Harris & Jones, 2018; Neves & Schyns, 2018). Leaders can, however, be a toxic influence on an organisation and the individuals within it. They can be motivated by narcissistic fantasies and ego-driven egocentricity rather than by altruistic or noble purpose (Franco et al., 2011; Thomson, 2009). Certain organisational contexts—such as those that are unstable, ambiguous, uncertain, with centralised discretionary power, or driven by policies that overemphasise performance measurement and competition—can enable, encourage, or compel bad leadership behaviours (Milley, 2017). Leadership can give power and agency to an elite few while cementing and romanticising hierarchies (Tourish, 2013).

If leaders want to grow their people, then the focus must be on the organisation and the capacities of individuals within it, not on the leader as central hero or dictator of a narrow range of acceptable professional learning. My own study of school leadership (Netolicky, 2018a, 2018b) found that school leaders can intentionally decide when to be visible and charismatic, and when to step back and empower others to lead. Leaders can resist stereotypes and create alternate narratives of leading, including by considering how best to support their staff through professional learning that makes a difference.

The constant cry for school improvement and the relentless accountability judgements from all angles—systems, media, community—have an impact on leadership of professional learning. Richard Niesche and Pat Thomson (2017) argue that "school leadership has increasingly been robbed of its educative purpose and is now ruled by school effectiveness and improvement discourses" (p. 203). Harmful side effects of accountability regimes, league tables, and an emphasis on external testing data, lead to teaching to the test, inequity, unrealistic measures of improvement, closing down of professional judgement, and stifling the capacity to innovate (Thomson, 2009). These side effects can leak into the realm of professional learning, as leaders in schools become more and more responsible for determining and delivering professional learning in their schools in order to support and develop staff. Meanwhile, school principals are desiring increasing amounts of freedom, power, and authority (Thomson, 2010), including in how they develop their staff.

George Gilchrist (2018) suggests that the first thing individual educators and schools should consider before making decisions around professional learning or designing a professional learning intervention is to know *where* you are as a school. I would argue, that even before asking *where* we are, it is necessary to know *who* we are. What is it that is at the very core of our education system, school, or practice? What do we believe, and what are our non-negotiables in terms of the education we are providing for our students? These questions are not simply answered, but a clear understanding of our purpose can be a solid foundation for deciding how to invest in building the capacity of those working in schools.

Leading from throughout the organisation

Principals are the focus of much research into school leadership, something that Peter Gronn (2009) calls a "curious and ironical tendency that should not go unremarked" (p. 314). The profile of the principalship continues to intensify, even amid cries for flatter, less hierarchical school structures within decentralised systems (Eacott, 2015). Perhaps we see a glut of research about principalship because principals are more easily accessed or identified by researchers for research purposes. Perhaps they are more willing to participate in research as they feel less vulnerable and more confident in what they have to say than those working at lower levels in school leadership and management. Or perhaps the focus on the principal is because of their role in setting the tone of the organisation, and having a clear influence on the professional learning culture of a school. Principals make decisions about how much time and money is to be invested in staff learning, and about what kinds of staff learning will be acknowledged, encouraged, and supported by the school. A principal can foreground and celebrate, or diminish and ignore, the learning of their staff. They control the extent to which their school is focused on monitoring and evaluation, or on support and development.

Middle leaders can take a leading role in professional learning in schools. These leaders are those with positions of responsibility beyond teachers leading initiatives or coaching peers, and not at the governance level of school executive or principalship. Many working in schools would suggest that those leading in the middle are a core part of the engine that powers school change. As head of faculty at three schools, I often felt like the filling in the sandwich between senior leadership and teachers, having to manage up and lead down at the same time. I was both the voice of school management—to my team, communicating and supporting school-wide reform and expectations—and also the voice of my team, advocating for their needs and protecting them from administrivia and accountability pressures as they went about their teaching. I was also immersed in classroom practice—mine and that of my team—and so well-placed to be not just a messenger, but also a driver of change. This experience is reflected in research into a project that explored 16 middle school leaders in England, in which Stoll et al. (2018) found that middle leaders are catalysts for improving teacher practice when they role model practice, champion improvement, provide constructive feedback, and build collaborative cultures within their teams.

Alma Harris et al. (2019) found that, while there has been steady scholarly interest in middle leadership in schools, the research base is limited and there remains a relatively low number of studies on middle leadership, compared to other topics within the field of educational leadership. This gap in the literature is reflected in practice in Australia, where there are professional standards for teachers and for principals, but no standards for those leading in the middle. When I reflect on the available AITSL National Professional Standards for Teachers and Principals, it is clear that there is a chasm between the 'lead teacher' standards and the principal standards. The lead teacher standards describe teachers who lead colleagues and processes; evaluate and revise teaching programs; monitor and appraise the use of teaching strategies; and initiate and lead the review of school policies and interventions. The principal standards focus on leadership and governance such as creating school culture; developing and implementing school improvement plans and policies; building the capacities of staff; allocating and managing resources; and evaluating the effects of change. Middle leaders seem to have been forgotten. They are betwixt the teacher who leads, and the principal charged with governing the school. The assumptions inherent in the standards about teachers at various career stages, and the gaping hole where middle leadership standards might be, are limitations of the Australian standards.

As middle leaders are simultaneously involved in teaching and leading they are more attuned to classroom learning than bureaucracy and governance, and in an excellent position to provide instructional leadership within schools (Grootenboer, 2018; Hargreaves et al., 2018). In their report on 'Leading from the middle: a school-based strategy for middle leaders in schools,' a professional development program for 57 middle leaders in New South Wales, Australia, Chris Day and Christine Grice (2019) found that middle leaders saw themselves as the bridge between the classroom and the boardroom. They report that central to middle leadership in schools that is effective in enacting change, is leadership of pedagogy that focuses on improving student learning.

Leading in the middle has been described as leading among peers, from within the group, rather than as the crusader out in front (Grootenboer, 2018) and as leadership in which middle leaders have influence over their own portfolio (Day & Grice, 2019). *Leading from the middle* takes the view that middle leaders are not a mere layer that connects the classroom to the boardroom, but "the heart and soul of leadership" who can "collaborate together purposefully, responsibly and transparently to develop strategies that will serve the children they know best" (Hargreaves et al., 2018, p. 127). *Leading beyond the middle* has been defined as middle leadership that has school-wide influence (Day & Grice, 2019). Middle leadership is different to principalship and there is a need to further support middle leaders such as heads of department, instructional coaches, curriculum coordinators, or specialist teachers, via resources and supportive school structures (Hargreaves et al., 2018).

Teacher leadership is another phenomenon that is increasingly seen as a key vehicle for school improvement; it empowers teachers, and contributes to school improvement and the spreading of good practice (Muijs & Harris, 2006), including in and through the field of professional learning. Teacher leaders can themselves be important resources for the learning of colleagues. The increase in teacher leader positions has been argued to be a result of school systems recognising that professional development offerings do not result in changed teacher behaviours in the classroom, and that internal, ongoing leadership such as coaching and mentoring by teacher leaders is more likely to have an impact (Katzenmeyer & Moller, 2009). *Teacher leadership*, however, is a problematic, ambiguous term that is used in various ways by different scholars, resulting in a confused field of research (Berg & Zoellick, 2019). Teacher leadership is often used to mean what I would call middle leadership—that is, formal leadership roles that teachers undertake with both management and pedagogical responsibilities, such as head of department—and also informal leadership roles such as coaching or setting up action research groups (Muijs & Harris, 2007). Teacher leaders are those who lead within and beyond the classroom; identify with and contribute to a community of teachers; influence others towards improved educational practice; and accept responsibility for achieving the outcomes of their leadership (Katzenmeyer & Moller, 2009). These can be veteran teachers, or younger and newly qualified teachers keen to exercise leadership. Teacher leaders obtain legitimacy and support for their leadership, have a range of objectives, and use various methods of leading including facilitating, coaching, evaluating, advocating, and negotiating (Berg & Zoellick, 2019). Teacher leadership is about leading as a practice, a *doing* of leadership, rather than assigned administrative duties or prescribed roles. It is about influence and impact.

Being teachers themselves, teacher leaders are hyper aware of teachers' stresses, needs, and constraints, including the limited time and effort they can devote to new practices (Nguyen & Hunter, 2018). Teacher leaders can leverage this knowledge and empathy, supporting other teachers in implementation and thereby easing school reforms into teachers' work lives (Nguyen & Hunter, 2018). Time needs to be set aside for teachers to meet to plan, discuss, organise, and lead initiatives, with those in and outside of their school contexts (Muijs & Harris, 2007). There is also no guarantee that teachers will accept leadership from teacher leaders, and tensions arise between collegiality and conflict, and teacher leaders feeling a loss of their teacher identity as they become to some degree like an administrator (Nguyen & Hunter, 2018).

Leadership from this ground to middle level requires collaborative cultures of trust and support, shared school vision, clear line management structures, strong leadership, and engagement in innovative forms of professional development (Muijs & Harris, 2006, 2007). Specifically, schools that embrace teacher leadership develop cultures in which leadership is not defined by role or title, but in which all are encouraged to initiate, lead, and hold one another accountable. Teachers need to feel able, supported to, and even expected to, participate in practices of leading.

One popular model of flatter leadership is *distributed leadership* (Gronn, 2010), in which organisational influence is not monopolised by one person, but shared around among a number of influential forces, or groups of individuals who come together interdependently to exert their influence jointly. This sounds good in theory as, rather than one authoritarian figure, there is a team of leaders who share the load and the work of leading. In my experience, distributed leadership in schools can empower a range of individuals to share leadership, especially when those individuals can effectively communicate and collaborate with one another and with their teams. I have also, however, seen it work badly. Sometimes a distributed approach means too many chefs in the proverbial school kitchen, with competing and inconsistent approaches and messages. It can mean a lack of clarity, and also an environment in which no one takes full responsibility, or where leaders think that they don't need to step forward, do particular work, or have a particular conversation, because surely someone else (one of the other leaders) will do it. Distributed leadership does not equal better leadership. It "is not a panacea or a blueprint or a recipe," "nor does it automatically improve performance" (Harris & Spillane, 2008, p. 33). Distributed leadership can be susceptible to maintaining hierarchies and subtly perpetuating embedded interests and structures (Youngs, 2017). Power relations of distributed leadership should be questioned and leadership considered as a practice (Youngs, 2017), rather than a new way of organising hierarchies. Sometimes clear hierarchical structures are effective and appropriate. What matters is the nature and quality of leadership practice, not necessarily that it is shared (Harris & Spillane, 2008).

Despite education's obsession with leadership and leading—from the highest leadership roles in education systems and schools, and increasingly, from the middle and the classroom—the professional learning culture of a school is not carried by one individual, or even a small group of enthusiasts. What improves teachers teaching is not "a collection of superstar teachers" but "interdependent colleagues who share and develop professional practices together" (Garmston & Wellman, 2013, p. 16). I have found the notion of *holonomy* a useful one for understanding the complexities of school leadership. Art Costa and Bob Garmston (2015) use this term to describe the complex and necessary tension between individual independence and group interdependence. They theorise a school as a holonomous culture in which individual teachers work within and respond to the school as an organic system. They base this on Arthur Koestler's work (1967, 1972) around the word *holon* as something that operates simultaneously as a part and a whole: autonomous and integrated, independent and interdependent, disparate and united. Koestler (1967) combines the Greek word *holos* meaning whole, and the suffix *on*, which indicates a particle or part; the holon is a part-whole. The metaphor of a tree and its branches illustrates the holistic, gestaltic, macro nature of things, at the same time as their interdependent partness: "It is as if the sight of the foliage of the entwined branches in a forest made us forget that the branches originate in separate trees" (Koestler, 1972, p. 240). In Costa and Garmston's application of holonomy to education, they conceptualise the teacher as individual, self-asserting, self-motivating, and self-modifying, but also influenced by the collective contextual norms, attitudes, values, and behaviours of their larger wholes (faculties, schools, districts). They describe each person as striving for a duality between a unique self-identity and connection with others. Holonomy poetically brings together the ecological symbiosis between the individual teacher (the parts) and the school or system (the whole). The implications for leadership of staff learning are that schools and their leaders need to address and honour the parts and the whole, the individual and the collective.

The collective efforts of a community of interdependent colleagues together result in an organisational learning culture and individual professional growth. Schools are likely to be improved through the cultivation of cultures of collaborative growth (Hargreaves & O'Connor, 2018). They should aim to create school-wide professional learning communities in which there are both clear and transparent leadership roles and responsibilities, and also cultures of learning and leading where peers hold one another accountable and individuals feel valued and confident to take initiative to lead within their spheres.

Context, culture, and trust

Identifying conditions conducive to professional learning is not the same as understanding the complexity and relational aspects of those conditions. The contexts in which teachers work are so variable that research cannot tell systems, schools, and teachers what to do, but research can identify which directions are likely to have the greatest benefits for students (Wiliam, 2016) and for teachers. Professional learning cannot be separated from wider contextual culture, so consideration of school context is key when considering leadership of professional learning and staff development. Leaders of education systems, and of schools, have an important role to play in the professional learning of teachers, but facilitating a staff learning culture is difficult. A safe and non-evaluative environment, in which power inequities are minimised, is central to a culture of learning, experimenting, and refining teaching practice. The paramount importance of school context in school change is a consideration for school as they undertake professional learning initiatives and make decisions about professional learning.

In terms of leading professional learning, it is important for schools to consider how they support the learning needs of staff as individual adult learners, while also utilising professional learning to move the school forward in its strategic priorities. As Jane Wilkinson and Stephen Kemmis (2015) note, education "is not simply a process of forming individuals. It is a process of forming societies, communities and other collectivities through the shaping of people's future practices" (pp. 355–356). Leadership of teachers and school leaders, and their learning, needs to consider social relationships among the group, that any organisational whole is made up of individuals who are bound together in ways that are dynamic and problematic (Eacott, 2015). Leaders develop school culture and shape how a community thinks and operates together. It is the job of leaders to provide a safe, coherent, and stable enough environment to protect and develop staff, while moving the organisation forward.

Trust is absolutely central in professional learning. Leaders play an important role in establishing the professional culture of an organisation, and can have a direct impact on individual staff. Ineffective, destructive, and counterproductive leadership can have negative impacts on individual staff and schools as organisations, including on stress, productivity, and wellbeing (Harris & Jones, 2018). Trust needs to be fostered, participants encouraged to recognise the need for improvement, and a culture of learning built. Systems and schools need to trust teachers to be professionals with the capacity for, commitment to, and execution of, teaching. Anthony Bryk and Barbara Schneider (2002) note that when school professionals trust each other and feel trusted, they feel safe to be vulnerable, experimental, and engaged in reform initiatives. A positive professional learning culture in schools means that staff review, enhance, and change their own roles, growing individuals and organisations simultaneously.

Trusting teachers means moving attention away from measured performance, surveillance, and compliance. It means moving towards capacity building, opportunities to improve, cultures of collaboration, and leveraging teacher voice in reform efforts. This means ensuring that the purpose of professional learning initiatives does not shift away from growth and towards surveillance and performance. In order to improve teachers' teaching and students' learning, education policies and practices would benefit from working from the assumption that teachers are capable, reflective practitioners with the capacity to grow. Schools as professional learning contexts benefit from being growth-focused, not accountability driven.

The role of research and data

We are operating in an education world in which evidence-based practice is promoted and sometimes expected, and in which the field of medicine is seen as a benchmark against which education should measure itself. Schools, school leaders, and teachers are increasingly expected to be research literate, to be informed by evidence in their decisions and practices, and to be assessed against a range of high stakes measures. There is also a high susceptibility to education fads (Jones, 2018), but it is no longer accepted that teachers try fads or ideas without an evidence base (Gilchrist, 2018). School leaders make decisions about where to invest in teacher learning, but there is so much going on in education that it's hard to know on what we should be focusing our time, resources, and energies.

Teachers and school leaders are often presented with arguments that begin with sweeping and unsubstantiated statements like 'the research says'. Often this is merely lip service to research, and statements are made with little understanding of scholarship. With education trends being propelled by popularity and pervasiveness, and conflicting bombardments about what should be happening in classrooms and schools, to whose word should educators listen? How might school leaders make decisions about where they invest in teacher professional learning?

Gary Jones (2018) reminds us that 'evidence' does not just mean research. It also encompasses:

- Data, facts, and figures generated at the school;
- Professional practitioner judgement; and
- The expertise, values, and concerns of stakeholders.

The education world is awash with data, and with expectations that teachers and schools use data to inform their practice. In the Australian context, the Gonski 2.0 report (Gonski et al., 2018) says that "timely and rich data will help teachers make responsive and informed decisions about how to most effectively support individual student growth and achievement" (p. 62). It adds that teachers need to "analyse and use data and evidence about student learning to select appropriate resources and activities to tailor teaching to meet the personalised learning needs of students" (p. 67). This Australian perspective reflects the global expectation that teachers and schools generate, store, analyse, and consider a range of qualitative and quantitative data to gauge student progress and make decisions on how to improve that progress through teaching, resourcing, and professional learning.

In schools, data can be used at various levels and in a multiplicity of ways, to inform decision making, teaching, learning, and governance. In the classroom, data-informed practice might look like formative assessment to improve student learning, or examining student work as a valuable form of professional learning. Action research is one iterative and ongoing data-informed process that involves forming an inquiry question, planning, generating data, and reflecting on results. A practitioner enquiry approach (Gilchrist, 2018) includes repeatedly collecting data around a group of learners, as a basis for collaboration, discussion, evaluation, and iteration. Laurenz Langer et al. (2016) emphasise the need to consider both process and context when using evidence to inform school change; they advocate for personalising any reform to context, culture, and the individuals involved, as well as building in evaluation from the outset. This way, when designing an intervention, leaders have thought about the questions: What will it look like if we are successful? How will we know the impact?

Among cries that teachers and schools need practices that are data-rich and evidence-informed, scholars and others are attempting to provide educators with quick and easy ways to utilise research evidence, or to ensure that teachers are using 'best practice.' Organisations that provide research publications and conferences include CollectiveED, based at Leeds Beckett University; the Centre for Evidence Management at Durham University, the Chartered College of Teaching, and ResearchED, all based in the UK. The resources and support provided by these kinds of organisations have the potential to be invaluable to the teaching profession. That many resources are open access helps teachers and school leaders who often cannot access research that exists behind a pay wall. The Education Endowment Foundation in the UK and Evidence for Learning in Australia are also producing reports on education research.

Some organisations, authors, and corporations offer simplified solutions to time poor teachers and schools looking for accessible research, and for professional learning based on understanding education research. One such example is John Hattie's (2009) *Visible Learning* work that has spread around the education world, spawning multiple books, posters, partnerships, and professional learning workshops. The Visible Learning website boasts a 'Hattie ranking' of 252 influences on student learning, links to buy a number of books, and a link to an online professional development program. On the one hand, the *Times Education Supplement* heralded this well-known example as the education holy grail and described Hattie as a near-messiah. On the other, it has been critiqued as pseudoscience (Bergeron & Rivard, 2017; Zhao, 2018), and questioned as an idea in education that has taken on unquestioned cult status (Eacott, 2017). A number of scholars have criticised Hattie's meta-meta-analytical research method and its usefulness in education (Simpson, 2017; Snook et al., 2009; Terhart, 2011; Wiliam, 2016), yet Visible Learning has become big professional learning business and is popular in schools around the world. The research behind Visible Learning can tell us something, but like all research it is limited. If policymakers, school leaders, or teachers are to base decisions on a particular set of research, the limitations need to be understood and the research applied with care and caution.

If professional learning is to make a difference in schools, those of us working in schools need to be able to make meaningful sense of the research upon which advice and claims are based. School leaders need to be careful of accepting simplified answers, laminated posters, and hierarchical lists of 'what (apparently, according to a particular method or expert) works' at face value. We need to consider our own professional judgement and the diversity of our contexts. We need to be willing to interrogate claims of 'research says' or 'what works.' We need to be wary of confident claims about research and its implications for our practice. School leaders and teachers need to be encouraged to ask questions of research such as: Where did the studied intervention work? For whom? Under what conditions? How many participants were in the study? From what school contexts? How were data generated? What were the ethical considerations and how were these dealt with? Those peddling 'what works' solutions or providing summaries of research can encourage teachers to draw back the curtain on the research on which those solutions or summaries are based.

Research matters, but context and the professional judgement of teachers matters, too. I agree with George Gilchrist (2018), who writes that,

> it is absolutely vital that we are informed by research and build on the experiences of others. But, it is just as important that we engage critically with such research and experience, to consider carefully what this means for us in our context (p. 131).

In the field of professional learning, this means being cautious before jumping on new bandwagons or at shiny offerings. It means considering the internal expertise of schools and systems, not always looking outside for easy solutions that can be bought. It means judicious, long term planning of staff development.

Leadership that resists policy and performativity

School leaders simultaneously navigate 'two wild horses' of education (Cody, 2019): measured externally imposed accountabilities and the moral, ethical, and holistic education of their students. They wrestle with data and mandates while doing their best to stay true to their school communities and serve the students in their care. School leaders are constrained by narrowing expectations, increasing pressures, and performative policy influences (Heffernan, 2018). Scott Eacott (2015) notes that the push for nebulous 'quality' in schools is usually measured against performance in standardised testing regimes, meaning that the quality argument is more often than not backward mapped into policy and subsequent planning documents. He adds that the imposition of quality performance measures is likely to lead to the pursuit of efficiency, constraining school leader autonomy rather than facilitating it. For instance, the behaviours of the three principals in Amanda Heffernan's research study (2018) were shaped by surveillance, achievement metrics, and external testing data, namely Australia's NAPLAN. In this environment, school leaders often become adept at playing the performance game, rather than at challenging policies and measures that constrain their leadership (Thomson, 2010).

There are snapshots, however, of principals who resist performative demands (e.g. Heffernan, 2018; Keddie et al., 2018), demonstrating that school leaders are social agents driven by social, moral, and ethical imperatives, rather than slaves to external or mandated expectations. As a former principal of two primary schools in Scotland, George Gilchrist (2018) writes about his own resistance to traditional educational hierarchies: "You are less likely to welcome interventions and changes imposed from outside of the school, which have not been shaped or adjusted taking account of your unique circumstances and context" (pp. 132–133). These are examples of moral accountability in which educators hold *themselves* to account for acting in accordance with their personal morals and values and professional ethics, rather than being driven by compliance. These behaviours reflect what Eric Hoyle and Mike Wallace (2007) call *principled infidelity*, in which teachers and school leaders do no opt out of or rebel against policy, but work round expectations, appearing to meet requirements. They conform to the expectations of education reform while holding firm on their beliefs of what matters most.

As the ever-increasing nature of professional demands on teachers and principals poses threats to their wellbeing (Hargreaves et al., 2019), resisting policy can mean leading in ways that focus on people and wellbeing as well as, or even instead of, meeting accountabilities and measures of outward success. This means more than adding staff yoga classes or meditation sessions. It means thinking deeply about solutions to teacher workload and considering what can be taken off teachers' plates when adding on more tasks, expectations, or accountabilities.

Spotlight on research: leadership for staff professional learning

During my PhD study I interviewed 11 school leaders. All 20 academic leaders at the Australian Pre-Kindergarten to Year 12 school were invited to participate; five executive leaders and six middle leaders agreed. The school leader participant group was made up of five women and six men. All 11 school leaders, including those at executive levels, taught one or more classes in addition to their leadership role. What follows is how these leader participants describe their leadership of teachers' learning. The themes that emerged were:

- Professional learning should honour context and people;
- Professional learning related to school change should happen at an appropriate pace; and
- Professional learning should be underpinned by a shared vision.

Each is explained below, using quotes from these leader participants.

Professional learning should honour context and people

These leaders were adamant that, when considering learning and change in schools, there needs to be a sensitivity to context as "no two places are the same." That is, any school decision or initiative "depends on the people that you're working with. It depends on the situation. It depends on where a school is at." Context matters immensely.

In terms of the specific coaching intervention that provided the context for this study, one leader expressed that they hoped that it was a catalytic context resulting in positive shifts in collaboration, reflection, and school culture. Their dream for the intervention was to "shift that critical mass and that critical mass generates momentum, then the snowball will get bigger and the snowball will get bigger and then we might have this vibrant professional space whereby we are prepared to" be open, vulnerable and continuously improving, together and individually. A middle leader used the metaphor of the coaching intervention being like oil in water. This leader said, "it's got to make a difference. To me it's like sort of oil in water. You're doing this, you're going out so what you've learned won't stay with you ... it's already moving out" beyond the individual and into the organisation. An executive leader described the coaching intervention as "a catalyst for a cultural shift" and four leaders felt that by its second pilot year there had already been a "qualitative shift" in school culture as a result of the coaching intervention and teachers' involvement in it.

The school leader participants of my PhD were mindful of the individuals in their school community as human beings with individual needs. Students, teachers, and parents were central to their decision making. Ten of the 11 school leaders explicitly discussed the student as the core of school business around which everything else should revolve and on which all school decisions should be based. Leading teachers and supporting their professional development is "about leading adult people such that you'll get better or optimal outcomes for kids." One leader remembered their first principal saying, "schools are ... about the students, and if you're not putting the students first ... then you need to find somewhere else to be." Another explained that the "students are the most important" driving factor in schools; the student is always "at the centre" in education. Those leading schools "should imagine a kid sitting in the corner of the room, and that's your child at school" and every decision "has to come back to them;" everything, including decisions about professional learning, must "benefit students." In the view of these leaders, the job of teachers, leaders, and schools is to make a difference, even a "little tiny difference," to the life of each "actual individual child." One leader spoke about "every kid, every single student" as having a "talent," and "the ultimate goal of education is to unlock that talent and to broaden its impact." As part of this close connection to students, the leaders in my study felt it was vital to continue to have a "direct relationship with kids." Leaders were "not prepared to give it up" but often "struggle to fit" relationships with students into their schedules. This aim of getting into classrooms and out into the yard was a difficult one to maintain in the busy life of a school leader, but one that was a grounding notion for these leaders, anchoring them in the purpose and humanity of their work.

Connecting with and understanding the staff at the school was also pivotal to these leaders' leadership of professional learning. Adult learning, one leader remarked, can't be top down because "you burn trust; you get everybody off side; they stop taking risks; they're not on board." Having "trust in people's capacity" needs to be balanced with making them "responsible for themselves." Teachers "are adults; they can make adult decisions" about their own learning and practice. Some of these leaders saw staff as having a "wealth of knowledge and experience that we just don't call on enough." "There's an incredible amount of expertise and knowledge in the staff here." People within teams and within the school are utilised to share internal expertise and push each other's work and thinking forward or in unexpected directions. Then, "if we don't have the skills in-house, let's get somebody in to teach us those skills that we need to know" or "take us through the process of thinking we need to do." Each team and each teacher is "distinctly different" so leading professional learning means knowing your context and also "knowing your staff."

Some leaders saw teacher wellbeing as explicitly linked to student learning. These leaders were aware that they needed to be "cognisant about" teachers, their beliefs, and their wellbeing. "So much in schools is focused on the students … but staff are also important because if the staff are not happy or feel they're supported" then there is an "impact on student learning." The argument of leaders was that, if the teachers are better, "the school's better and so therefore the students gain so much more." One leader saw their job as to help teachers to realise "what the benefits to the students are" and "what the benefits to themselves as an educator are." Leaders are aware of their need to "support people's health and wellbeing" and to "ensure that they don't burn out and that they feel good about themselves as workers" in order to ensure quality, satisfied teachers, and consequently well-looked-after students who are helped to achieve to the best of their ability. One leader asked themselves,

> How do you get a school to where you want it without burning out your teachers, without asking too much, accepting they've got a life outside of school and a family and that to do the best job they can they actually have to have that life balance satisfaction in place?

In an attempt to address this, they try to make sure that staff are "doing the right work and not doing extra work."

These school leaders were constantly navigating the holonomous tension between individual student or staff needs and the needs of the organisation. Patrick Duignan (2012) calls this the tension between common good and individual good, and Scott Eacott (2015) calls it individualism versus collectivism. All 11 leaders explicitly identified and discussed the importance and challenges of balancing organisational vision and direction with individuals and their own learning and life journeys. "Almost every difficult decision is that balance between the individual and the collective."

Professional learning related to school change should happen at an appropriate pace

All 11 leaders in my PhD study were focused on the notion of continuous improvement for themselves, their teams, their staff, and their students. They realised, however, that schools are organisations that "move really quickly," full of "busyness," "complexity," and "so many things on the go at once." Like many educators, these leaders had seen educational trends "come around … repackaged with a different name." Many veteran teachers will attest to the constant merry-go-round of reforms in education. Much like the famous Sun Tzu line that "if you wait by the river long enough, the bodies of your enemies will float by," many teachers feel that if you wait in your classroom long enough, the next educational reform will pass you by and another will take its place, such is the rate of change in education. These leaders were therefore wary of "flip-flopping from good idea to good idea, because there's hundreds of good ideas out there educationally." One gave an example to which many of us working in schools can relate; they knew of a leader who would return to school after attending a professional development course to "the looks on staff faces … and they think, 'Oh here we go again, it's going to be another idea, something else to change.'" Leaders in my study saw current school environments, where innovation fatigue is rife and the pace is relentless, can "push a lot of people out of their real area of comfort." Change in schools therefore needs to be "embedded in research and deliberate," not knee-jerk fast or unthinkingly adopting the "next thing." These leaders knew that real school change "takes a lot of time," can "be a slow journey," and is "an evolution not a revolution."

Yet while they recognised the need to approach change slowly and deliberately, these leaders did not always see going slow as an option. In the current environment of public performance and external accountabilities, they felt compelled to be always moving forward. A tension for these leaders was "finding the right speed at which to push" their staff because "while you want to create a culture of really solid learning that creates change for the better," this aim is not always compatible with the reality of teachers' professional lives. There was a constant need to find the "fine balance" between "going forward" and "creating a strong culture for the better, of greater student learning, of greater professional satisfaction," with slowing down enough to "bring people along." Five of the 11 school leaders interviewed talked explicitly about forward momentum and "moving [people, groups, change] forward." They did not feel as though they could make excuses for stagnating, or use the excuse of "Oh, look we are too busy…. so let's just stop, let's just not do this," because "you'll always be busy." Leaders felt pressure to avoid inertia and keep individuals, teams, and the organisation "moving forward" positively and dynamically.

Professional learning should be underpinned by a shared vision

The notion of a shared, coherent vision makes an appearance in much literature on school leadership, and it was a common theme among these leaders. All 11 leaders discussed the importance of alignment between organisational vision and decision making around professional learning.

Four leaders talked specifically about the need for vision to be "shared" by the school community. This requires "shared understanding" and "collective buy-in" in order to be effective. Four leaders aimed to co-create vision, "growing that collaboratively with teachers and also with important stakeholders," and being transparent about vision with staff. "If I want them to see the bigger picture then I have to make sure that they know what the bigger picture is." Any school-wide intervention that required professional learning of staff needed to be aligned with visionary purpose and balanced with a realistic view of teachers' lives. The challenge for leaders was to "empower others to live the vision," to facilitate the understanding, living, and enacting of that vision by the school and its community. Leaders saw vision as aligned with school context, but also be research-based and "data-influenced." "In education we've got a responsibility to keep up with research" because it "has changed our profession and therefore should change us as leaders." It gives educators a "language" and a "science" for the profession "and that means we can empower both ourselves and our learners." Schools should look to "broader sets of data" than "traditional external data sources" to gauge whether change is "having any impact for students."

Leaders commented that without clear articulation of vision, strategic planning around vision, and working towards shared understanding of the vision, a good idea might happen briefly but then "die after you die or leave." The organisation would then move "on to the next good idea." In order for the shared vision to effect change and be sustainable, it is "really, really important" that there is a cascade of vision from organisation to team to individual, so that teachers' vision and action "ties back to our vision." Leaders used the metaphor of staff getting on the "train" or "bus" together; "we've all signed off on" and "we all work towards" that vision in clearly defined roles, "clear structures" and strategic plans at organisation, team, and individual level. "And everything that we do comes back to that plan." One leader saw their role as "coaching" and "empowering" others to develop their own personal "vision within that vision" so that each individual has their own vision aligned with the larger organisational vision. "Using that idea of vision-based mission-based leadership" the leader hoped "to get everyone on board … moving towards the goal and owning the goal and being part of the journey."

A micro example of vision aligned with leadership and practice was found in leaders' responses to the studied coaching intervention, which focused on lesson observation and coaching conversations as a way to build professional culture and improve teaching and teacher awareness of and reflection on practice. Leaders were drawn to support the intervention because of their alignment with its purpose, resonance with the school context, and a desire for voice and impact. The intervention came out of the school strategic plan and was initiated by the principal, but it was me as researcher-teacher-and-facilitator and the team of classroom teachers who enacted the intervention's early years. We also developed recommendations to the governing board of the school about the direction the work could take in the future. The school leaders were not directly involved in the coaching intervention but viewed it from a strategic perspective. One executive leader described the intervention as "trusting that people have those capacities within them, just providing them with the opportunities to explore and reflect on that in real ways." Another explained that it fits well with my idea that when I want to learn I want to be involved in the process, so it is a collaborative process, as opposed to someone telling you what to do. You have to figure out yourself from the evidence and it is evidence-based.

This leader added that "it does mean that teachers are setting their own goals and being self-directed learners, taking ownership of that, so that all fits very well with my own beliefs about learning."

At an organisation or school level, the vision and strategic direction was seen by one leader as a "lighthouse." It represented the beaconic direction towards which the leader endeavoured to steer their team, including "the vision and the goals that we share," "big picture stuff" which is "like an umbrella" under which teams and teachers fit their own learning. Another used the metaphor of a tree that continues to shape my own thinking about leadership ever since. It's an image that powerfully encapsulates what it means to lead the organisation or team, and concurrently honour, support, and grow each individual. This leader explained that they saw the solid trunk of the tree as being the overarching foundational team or organisational vision, with the organisational vision's roots grounding the tree. Team and individual visions and journeys branch off from the shared trunk, connected and anchored to it but growing in their own organic directions. The tree metaphor presents the school or team vision as "overarching but it's collectively drawn, so that it's not imposed on your staff, and that's what you're working towards, but you've also got the sense of the individual."

Spotlight on practice: overseeing staff professional learning in a school

At the time of writing, my school role is titled Dean of Research and Pedagogy. The 'research' part of the role is concerned with developing a research-informed professional learning culture of continual improvement, data generation, and analysis; a research base and systematic methodologies of the organisation; data generation and analytics; executing evidence-based strategic initiatives; and overseeing and developing research and innovation frameworks. The 'pedagogy' part of my role sees me overseeing teaching practice across the Pre-Kindergarten to Year 12 school. This includes overseeing the professional learning agenda and staff development, overseeing teacher action research projects, supporting our staff doing postgraduate study, leadership development, coaching teachers and leaders, and refining performance and growth processes. In this role, I am charged with overseeing our teacher coaches, mentor teachers, teacher leader action research projects, and other staff involved in our differentiated internal professional learning model. Below I explain the way I approach overseeing the professional learning of staff, in practice in my Australian school.

Overseeing professional learning: where to begin?

In 2017, my first year of what was then a new role at the school, I began by mapping out how I was going to address the multiple aspects of my role in a school with about 1500 students from Pre-Kindergarten to Year 12, and about

140 teachers. What was my underlying strategy? What were the deliverables? Who were the key stakeholders? At the end of each year, how might I know I had been successful? What evidence of my own influence might I see if I was being successful in nudging the ever-nebulous school culture? I wrote a two-year strategic plan (a working document that I revisit regularly) and put some measures for myself in place. Each year I report back on staff professional learning for the year, and I use data such as staff surveys to plan professional learning for the year ahead.

I wrote a professional learning policy for the school (we didn't have one) that includes a rationale, definition, principles, and practices, making clear staff expectations and the decision making frame for approvals of professional learning for teaching staff. I additionally launched a new professional learning application process that required staff to provide rationales for their requested professional learning, as well as proper costings, including relief costs. I manage an intranet page that shares information related to professional learning, including a calendar, notices, processes, and forms.

A focus on growth

My school is focused on the growth and development of its staff, and so I base my decisions as a school leader on a belief in the capacity of everyone in the school community to grow and improve, and the positive presupposition that staff are committed to their ongoing learning and development. Each member of teaching staff has the right and responsibility to develop professionally, and the school has the responsibility to support the development of our staff as professionals through ongoing professional learning. This is about supporting staff in being self-efficacious, empowered individuals in control of their own professional growth and development, and so the focus of professional learning is on those learning opportunities that serve individual roles, team foci, and organisational priorities.

The school supports professional learning because we know it strengthens individuals and the organisation, and ultimately improves our ability to best serve our students and community, including the academic success of our students. We especially consider collaborative learning opportunities through modes such as staff days, team or group learning events, and sending groups of staff to courses or conferences in order to facilitate ongoing conversation and collaboration after their return. The impact on classes missed is considered in all professional development applications, as student learning remains our core work; this shouldn't be compromised. We also ensure that we harness the internal expertise of our staff in professional learning, as well as what experts can bring to our context. When inviting external experts such as consultants or academics to conduct professional learning or work with staff, we tend to build sustained, ongoing partnerships rather than offer one-off sessions.

A focus on growth means school leaders need to be listening to the voices of staff. Designing meaningful professional learning involves a lot of listening and a lot of seeking feedback, including from dissenting voices. I once had a school leader say to me: "Don't water the rocks." They meant that I should focus my attentions on the 'plants,' those staff who were early adopters or showing signs of embracing the incoming change. It does make sense to build a critical mass of those enthusiastic or accepting of change in schools, but I have found that it is also important to listen carefully and openly to those objecting to or resisting change, those who some might consider immovable 'rocks.' What are their arguments? How could we adjust what we are doing to make this meaningful for them? I constantly generate data on the success of my professional learning work, such as through focus groups and surveys, in order to ensure that the school's professional learning opportunities are responding to staff needs.

Differentiating staff development

Professional learning is for all staff, not just for those who are keen to apply for plenty of external professional development or volunteer for internal opportunities. As a result of the coaching intervention (piloted in 2013 and 2014, and then embedded for all teaching staff from 2015–2017), the school had implemented a three-year cycle for teachers and school leaders, with coaching at its core. Each year, staff were assigned to the process they were due to complete, based on a chronological cycle. In the first year of employment at the school, teaching staff undertook a rigorous probation process. The next three years then involved a linear cycle as follows.

- Year 1: Coaching cycle around teaching practice with a trained teacher coach (modelled on the coaching intervention).
- Year 2: Coaching cycle around teaching practice with a trained teacher coach (modelled on the coaching intervention).
- Year 3: Reflection and performance review with their line manager around their role.

This three-year cycle was then repeated: two years of non-judgemental coaching followed by a more formal manager-led process in the third year. This school-based process was in addition to in-school and external professional learning. Each year staff also had a reflection and goal setting conversation with their line manager, which functioned as an important check-in for the manager and a key feedback process for the staff member.

The above processes were carefully designed and aimed to engender trust, build capacity, and provide support, while also facilitating a relationship between person and manager around performance, development, and needs. While they were founded on the above-explained belief that all staff are capable professionals who have the capacity and the will to grow professionally; they were additionally underpinned by an organisational expectation that each member of staff will endeavour to improve, no matter how good they already are. Data, coaching, collaboration, mentoring, and self-reflection were all tools embedded into these processes.

Yet, despite the best intentions of these processes, and their basis in research, some staff have felt that the school-based development processes had not met their needs, or had not resulted in meaningful learning. We had some staff who didn't feel that coaching met their needs or who were frustrated by the linear and inflexible nature of the cycle. We had leaders who wanted more say in tailoring staff internal professional learning and in their own leadership development. As I worked in this space and generated staff feedback around their experiences, I began to wonder: How might school-based professional development be differentiated to meet the needs, aspirations, and career stages of staff? This question led to the recent development of a differentiated, negotiated model of internal professional growth, to replace the previous linear cyclical model.

In 2018 we launched a new way of thinking about our internal professional learning processes: negotiated professional learning pathways. Teachers and school leaders now use the annual goal setting conversation as an opportunity to negotiate with their manager a choice from a number of options. These currently include:

- *Coaching around practice or role* with a teacher trained in cognitive coaching and GROWTH coaching; involves using low inference data for reflection and capacity building within a confidential and trusting space; leaders can opt to be coached by a peer or other leader.
- *Working with an expert or mentor teacher* who acts as a kind of classroom consultant; might include team teaching and mentoring with specific advice around classroom practice.
- *A formal reflection and feedback process with their line manager* (every 3–4 years).
- An internally-designed *leadership development program* for aspirant or early career leaders; includes leadership profiles, school leaders running sessions, and a leadership project that addresses an area of need within the school.
- One of a number of *professional learning groups*, bringing staff together from across the school to engage in scholarly literature, reflection, collaboration, and shared practice. Topics are offered each year from which staff can choose.

Middle and senior leaders have a slightly different range of options for the first point above: coaching. They can negotiate to be coached by a peer, another leader from the within school, or an external coach or mentor. Unlike the teachers, who are coached around their teaching practice, leaders are likely to be coached around their leadership. This model works in part because all leaders are trained in coaching and can therefore coach one another. Executive leaders including the principal are coached by an external executive coach. The differentiation of coaching for teachers, middle leaders, and executive leaders reflects findings that show that senior leaders prefer being coached by external executive coaches and middle leaders prefer being coached by internal coaches (van Nieuwerburgh, 2016). This also reflects the increasing confidentiality and sensitivity of leadership issues for leaders in more senior positions.

Additionally, leaders at my school attend coaching training and a once-a-term leadership forum, a cheese-and-wine event that brings together all of our school leaders, from coaches and head of year, to heads of faculty and the executive leadership group. This is an opportunity to connect the strategy of the school with the operational and relational work of our leaders. The evenings run from

5pm–7pm, with 5pm–5.30pm being a time for arrival and mingling, 5.30pm–6.30pm being a time for the main event of the evening, and leaders welcome to remain from 6.30pm–7pm to mix with one another and talk with any presenter or guest speaker. After the first two years, we opened up the leadership forums to all staff, based in the belief that leading is a behaviour not a title. Some leadership forums have been run using internal expertise from the leaders in the room. These have included sessions on, for example, effective school leadership and strategic planning. They have also included keynote or workshop style presentations from international scholars, including Dylan Wiliam, Pasi Sahlberg, Christian van Nieuwerburgh, and Eric Sheninger. Bringing experts into the school, and having them speak to our context, meant that their words and points connected more strongly with the people in the room. Staff enjoyed the collaborative experience of hearing them speak, together, so conversations have continued well after each presentation finished. We have also run forums as panels, such as with local principals. Our leadership forum is one example of a way to engage teachers and leaders in current conversations around education, and with research and researchers. Creating these kinds of crucibles of collaboration, and following up with books or articles that build upon the presentations, has been one way to nudge people's thinking, especially when presenters are provocative or challenging.

All staff continue to complete their yearly reflection and goal setting conversation with their line manager. In order to support this work, all our school leaders, many of whom have previously completed the cognitive coaching foundation course, undertake GROWTH coaching training. This training helps them to guide and enhance the goal setting of the people they manage, and it supports our organisational belief (based in research and knowledge of our own context) that coaching is a powerful vehicle for building individual, collaborative and organisational capacity. We continue to provide additional leadership support and development.

The negotiated professional learning pathways do not cover everything that our staff do to develop themselves and others. All managers regularly check-in on the performance of their staff; they do not wait until the rigorous formal process rolls around. We have staff who mentor pre-service teachers, contribute to professional associations, attend and present at conferences, write textbooks, or complete postgraduate study. The above school-based options do, however, provide a more flexible suite of alternatives that honour where our staff are at in their career journeys. We continue to ask for honest feedback from staff as we seek to find ways to serve our students, staff, and the shared purpose of the organisation.

Engaging staff in research

Engaging in research, and in discussions and explorations about research, can help teachers to interrogate their beliefs and bring together science, evidence, and systematic thinking with their praxis (wisdom of practice). Having a person (me!) dedicated to the curation, generation, and communication of research supports everyone from the classroom to the boardroom in making better decisions. A role dedicated to raising the profile and practice of research helps a school to remain agile in response to current educational research; evidence-informed and systematic in its methods; proactive in its processes and communications; and keenly focused on its strategic impacts within the wider context of the global education world. My adjunct position at a university helps to keep me current as I have access to research literature behind the pay wall. I also keep the staff professional reading library current in order to provide staff with the opportunity to engage with current research. I promote books to staff, or distribute them to staff I think might benefit from particular texts.

Since my first year in this role, I have published a regular document that I called a 'research report' to all staff. The report intends to provide all staff —not just teachers—access to current thinking, research, and writing, around education. Across the year the report provides resources that range from academic and theoretical, to popular and easily accessible, including podcasts and vlogs. These resources are relevant to our specific school context, including to various sub-schools, faculties, and strategic priorities. The selected readings are a small selection rather than a comprehensive collection. Staff are encouraged to dip in and out according to their personal and professional interests. I have been interested to note those people who have provided positive feedback about the report; many are operational or administration staff who have appreciated being able to immerse themselves in, or dip into, educational thinking, and have this shared in an accessible way. Making research accessible to all democratises the community and empowers everyone to have conversations around education. It has incited many corridor conversations, as well as more formal ones. I additionally use the school's blog as a vehicle for referencing current research in order to model how research can inform the thinking of educators and schools.

Key takeaways

- Leadership is often represented as visionary, charismatic, heroic, or selfless, with a focus on the positive aspects and outcomes. Leaders can, however, be damaging, negative, and toxic. They can also choose positive alternative ways of leading.
- School leadership is overrun by accountability measures of school effectiveness and the push for school improvement. Leaders can, however, choose to resist performative pressures in ways that benefit their school contexts.
- School leadership scholarship and practice is often focused on the principal, but benefits from a broader focus including on middle and teacher leadership.
- Middle and teacher leaders can have significant impact and can be key players in the professional learning context of a school.
- Leading professional learning means building trust and considering context and a school-wide culture of learning.
- Professional learning can be differentiated for the varied needs, goals, experience, and career stages of staff, especially if it is to shift beliefs and practices.

- School leaders can consider evidence to inform their decision making around professional learning. Evidence includes data, facts, and figures generated at the school; professional practitioner judgement; and the expertise, values, and concerns of stakeholders.
- School leaders need to be wary of oversimplified professional learning solutions that promote a 'what works' approach. Professional judgement and the diversity of school contexts should be considered. School leaders can ask: What can and does this research or evidence tell us? What can't or doesn't it tell us?

References

Berg, J. H., & Zoellick, B. (2019). Teacher leadership: Toward a new conceptual framework. *Journal of Professional Capital and Community*, 4(1), 2–14.

Bergeron, P. J., & Rivard, L. (2017). How to engage in pseudoscience with real data: A criticism of John Hattie's arguments in visible learning from the perspective of a statistician. *McGill Journal of Education/Revue Des Sciences De L'éducation De McGill*, 52(1), 237–246.

Bryk, A., & Schneider, B. (2002). *Trust in schools: A core resource for improvement*. New York: Russell Sage Foundation.

Cody, R. (2019). Riding two wild horses: Leading Australian schools in an era of accountability. In D. M. Netolicky, J. Andrews, & C. Paterson (Eds.). *Flip the system Australia: What matters in education* (pp. 198–203). Abingdon: Routledge.

Costa, A. L., & Garmston, R. J. (2015). *Cognitive coaching: Developing self-directed leaders and learners*. London: Rowman & Littlefield.

Day, C., & Grice, C. (2019). *Investigating the influence and impact of leading from the middle: A school-based strategy for middle leaders in schools*. Sydney: University of Sydney.

Duignan, P. (2012). *Educational leadership: Together creating ethical learning environments*. New York: Cambridge University Press.

Eacott, S. (2015). The principalship, autonomy, and after. *Journal of Educational Administration and History*, 47(4), 414–431.

Eacott, S. (2017). School leadership and the cult of the guru: The neo-Taylorism of Hattie. *School Leadership & Management*, 37(4), 413–426.

Eraut, M. (2012). Developing a broader approach to professional learning. In A. Mc Kee & M. Eraut (Eds.). *Learning trajectories, Innovation and identity for professional development* (pp. 21–46). Dordrecht: Springer.

Franco, Z. E., Blau, K., & Zimbardo, P. J. (2011). Heroism: A conceptual analysis and differentiation between heroic action and altruism. *Review of General Psychology*, 15(2), 99–113.

Garmston, R. J., & Wellman, B. (2013). *Adaptive schools: A sourcebook for developing collaborative groups* (2nd ed.). Lanham, MD: Rowman & Littlefield.

Gilchrist, G. (2018). *Practitioner enquiry: Professional development wit impact for teachers, schools and systems*. Abingdon: Routledge.

Gonski, D., Arcus, T., Boston, K., Gould, V., Johnson, W., O'Brien, L., ... Roberts, M. (2018). *Through growth to achievement: The report of the review to achieve educational excellence in Australian schools*. Canberra: Commonwealth of Australia.

Gronn, P. (2009). Immaculate consummation: Learning meets leadership. *International Journal of Leadership in Education: Theory and Practice*, 12(3), 311–318.

Gronn, P. (2010). Leadership: Its genealogy, configuration, and trajectory. *Journal of Educational Administration and History*, 42(4), 405–435.

Grootenboer, P. (2018). *The practices of school middle leadership: Leading professional learning*. Singapore: Springer.

Hargreaves, A., & O'Connor, M. T. (2018). *Collaborative professionalism: When teaching together means learning for all.* Thousand Oaks: Corwin.

Hargreaves, A., Shirley, D., Wangia, S., Bacon, C., & D'Angelo, M. (2018). *Leading from the middle: Spreading learning, well-being, and identity across Ontario.* Ontario: Council of Ontario Directors of Education.

Hargreaves, A., Wangia, S., & O'Connor, M. (2019). Flipping their lids: Teachers' wellbeing in crisis. In D. M. Netolicky, J. Andrews, & C. Paterson (Eds.). *Flip the system Australia: What matters in education* (pp. 93–104). Abingdon: Routledge.

Harris, A., & Jones, M. (2018). The dark side of leadership and management. *School Leadership & Management, 38*(5), 475–477.

Harris, A., Jones, M., Ismail, N., & Nguyen, D. (2019). Middle leaders and middle leadership in schools: Exploring the knowledge base (2003–2017). *School Leadership & Management, 39* (3–4), 255–277.

Harris, A., & Spillane, J. (2008). Distributed leadership through the looking glass. *Management in Education, 22*(1), 31–34.

Hattie, J. A. (2009). *Visible learning: A synthesis of 800+ meta-analyses on achievement.* Abingdon: Routledge.

Heffernan, A. (2018). *The principal and school improvement: Theorising discourse, policy, and practice.* Singapore: Springer.

Hoyle, E., & Wallace, M. (2007). Educational reform: An ironic perspective. *Educational Management Administration & Leadership, 35*(1), 9–25.

Jones, G. (2018). *Evidence-based school leadership and management: A practical guide.* London: Sage.

Katzenmeyer, M., & Moller, G. (2009). *Awaking the sleeping giant: Helping teachers develop as leaders* (3rd). Thousand Oaks: Corwin.

Keddie, A., Gobby, B., & Wilkins, C. (2018). School autonomy reform in Queensland: Governance, freedom and the entrepreneurial leader. *School Leadership & Management, 38*(4), 378–394.

Koestler, A. (1967). *The ghost in the machine.* London: Arkana.

Koestler, A. (1972). Beyond atomism and holism: The concept of the holon. In T. Shanin (Ed.). *The rules of the game: Cross-disciplinary essays on models in scholarly thought* (pp. 192–232). London: Tavistock.

Langer, L., Tripney, J., & Gough, D. (2016). *The science of using science: Researching the use of research evidence in decision-making.* London: EPPI-Centre, Social Science Research Unit, UCL Institute of Education, University College London.

Milley, P. (2017). Maladministration in education: Towards a typology based on public records in Canada. *Educational Management Administration & Leadership, 45*(3), 466–483.

Muijs, D., & Harris, A. (2006). Teacher led school improvement: Teacher leadership in the UK. *Teaching and Teacher Education, 22*(8), 961–972.

Muijs, D., & Harris, A. (2007). Teacher leadership in (in) action: Three case studies of contrasting schools. *Educational Management Administration & Leadership, 35*(1), 111–134.

Netolicky, D. M. (2018a). Redefining leadership in schools: The Cheshire Cat as unconventional metaphor. *Journal of Educational Administration and History, 51*(2), 149–164.

Netolicky, D. M. (2018b). The visible-invisible school leader: Redefining heroism and offering alternate metaphors for educational leadership. In O. Efthimiou, S. T. Allison, & Z. E. Franco (Eds.). *Heroism and wellbeing in the 21st century: Applied and emerging perspectives* (pp. 133–148). New York: Routledge.

Neves, P., & Schyns, B. (2018). With the bad comes what change? The interplay between destructive leadership and organisational change. *Journal of Change Management, 18*(2), 91–95.

Nguyen, T. D., & Hunter, S. (2018). Towards an understanding of dynamics among teachers, teacher leaders, and administrators in a teacher-led school reform. *Journal of Educational Change, 19*(4), 539–565.

Niesche, R., & Thomson, P. (2017). Freedom to what ends? School autonomy in neoliberal times. In D. Waite & I. Bogotch (Eds.). *The Wiley International handbook of educational leadership* (pp. 193–206). Hoboken: Wiley.

Simpson, A. (2017). The misdirection of public policy: Comparing and combining standardised effect sizes. *Journal of Education Policy*, *32*(4), 450–466.

Snook, I., O'Neill, J., Clark, J., O'Neill, A. M., & Openshaw, R. (2009). Invisible learnings? A commentary on John Hattie's book: Visible learning: A synthesis of over 800 meta-analyses relating to achievement. *New Zealand Journal of Educational Studies*, *44*(1), 93–106.

Stoll, L., Brown, C., Spence-Thomas, K., & Taylor, C. (2018). Teacher leadership within and across professional learning communities. In A. Harris, M. Jones, & J. B. Huffman (Eds.). *Teachers leading educational reform: The power of professional learning communities* (pp. 51–71). Abingdon: Routledge.

Terhart, E. (2011). Has John Hattie really found the holy grail of research on teaching? An extended review of Visible Learning. *Journal of Curriculum Studies*, *43*(3), 425–438.

Thomson, P. (2009). *School leadership: Heads on the block?* Abingdon: Routledge.

Thomson, P. (2010). Headteacher autonomy: A sketch of a Bourdieuian field analysis of position and practice. *Critical Studies in Education*, *51*(1), 5–20.

Tourish, D. (2013). *The dark side of transformational leadership: A critical perspective*. New York: Routledge.

van Nieuwerburgh, C. (2016). Towards a philosophy of coaching. In C. van Nieuwerburgh (Ed.). *Coaching in Professional Contexts* (pp. 249–255). London: Sage.

Wiliam, D. (2016). *Leadership for teacher learning: Creating a culture where all teachers improve so that all students succeed*. Moorabbin: Hawker Brownlow Education.

Wilkinson, J., & Kemmis, S. (2015). Practice theory: Viewing leadership as leading. *Educational Philosophy and Theory*, *47*(4), 342–358.

Youngs, H. (2017). A critical exploration of collaborative and distributed leadership in higher education: Developing an alternative ontology through leadership-as-practice. *Journal of Higher Education Policy and Management*, *39*(2), 140–154.

Zhao, Y. (2018). *What works may hurt: Side effects in education*. New York: Teachers College Press.

Conclusion
What next in professional learning

As this book has shown, professional learning is an area of worldwide focus in the field of education. It exists in an education landscape in which policies and metrics encourage teachers and schools to focus on performing well in league tables or looking good on glossy brochures. The linking of teacher professional learning to student outcomes, teacher standards, and educational leadership, has left room for professional learning to become big business, propelled by corporate enterprise looking to make money out of the provision of professional development.

Constant short-termism results in education always chasing the next big thing. As Dylan Wiliam (2018) writes, "we need to stop looking for the next big thing and instead focus on doing the last big thing properly" (p. 118). In this book, research literature, empirical data, and practitioner lived experience come together to show that the ways in which educators interact with professional learning are highly individualised, not one-size-fits-all. Professional learning that transforms teachers' and school leaders' beliefs and practices can happen in diverse ways and in a variety of sometimes unexpected contexts.

Teachers, school leaders, system leaders, and researchers can best invest their time and resources in ongoing forms of professional learning that involve intentionality, clear structures, partnerships, meaningful collaboration, rich conversation, rigorous reflection, and carving out time and space for the learning of educators working in schools.

Below I outline five foci we would benefit from foregrounding in the planning and implementation of professional learning for teachers and school leaders:

- Consider identity and humanity;
- Offer voice and choice;
- Focus on context, culture, and relationships;
- Enable collaboration that is rigorous, purposeful, and sometimes uncomfortable;
- Broaden our definition of professional learning; and
- Invest time, money, and resources.

Consider identity and humanity

Transformational professional learning is that which results in learners being changed by their experiences in ways that positively impact their knowing, doing, and being. As this book reveals, professional learning deeply involves each teacher's or school leader's conceptions of self. We need to consider identity in the context of professional learning. Ivor Goodson (1991) writes that the personal in teaching is irrevocably linked to practice; that "it is as if the teacher *is* her or his practice" (p. 141). He positions teacher practice as the maximum point of vulnerability for teachers, and their greatest source of anxiety and insecurity. Schools would benefit from operating with an awareness of the vulnerability and anxiety of teachers with regard to opening their classrooms.

Teachers are continuous and lifelong learners, and every school has, as part of its core purpose, the care, security, and recognition of the importance of its teachers (Senge, 2012). Schools can allow and encourage their staff to be vulnerable and take risks, without punitive consequences. They can provide support and challenge, based in the belief that educators have the internal capacity for reflection and growth. This approach sits in opposition to punitive or performative schemes, which are based on keeping educators and schools accountable to externally imposed, numerically-measured standards, rather than nurturing teachers, leaders, and schools through growth-focused professional learning that operates from a starting point of accepting teachers as reflective professionals with the capacity to improve.

Teaching encompasses constant decision making, complex webs of theory and practice, and emotional work. Professional learning that ignores this complexity and treats teachers as technicians who implement new sets of behaviours disparate from their contexts are ineffective in changing practice (Timperley, 2008). It seems beyond obvious to say that we need to consider the teachers in our schools as humans, but so often education policy and school improvement practices focus on teachers as objects, subjects, or data points.

Professional learning should consider tensions in relationships, particularly as a result of imbalance of authority or confusion of purpose. These can interrupt professional learning and lead instead to inauthentic performance or forced compliance. Professional learning is a situated social practice and collective process profoundly influenced by environment and by social networks in personal and professional contexts. It is a human endeavour with all the emotional and relational complexities that entails.

Voice, choice, and space

Teacher voice is stifled by national and school compliance cultures (Keddie, 2017). Teachers in the USA, for instance, have limited influence in crucial areas of school decision making (Darling-Hammond et al., 2009). While there are those who do resist, those who do not toe the accountability line or play the compliance game can be pushed to the sidelines or pushed out of the profession (Ball, 2016). Often there is a scattergun approach to professional learning in which a bunch of educators are sat in a room, hall, or auditorium in order to 'have PD done to them' as I have often heard it called in my discussions with colleagues. Here professional learning is treated as a fix to a teacher problem or a prescription to an ailment.

Effective professional learning involves a balance of teacher voice and system coherence (Campbell et al., 2017). Christian van Nieuwerburgh (2016) advocates *democratic voluntary involvement* in coaching initiatives, which can transfer to professional learning more broadly. That is, each member of staff has the opportunity to participate, but also choice about their involvement. Ann Lieberman et al. (2017) identify choice and self-direction as key elements of successful adult learning. In their work with 4,300 educators across 840 professional development projects in Ontario, the authors conclude that students, teachers, and the teaching profession, benefit from enabling teachers to choose, organise, and lead professional development. They found that valuing and supporting teachers to take charge of their own professional learning is vital. They suggest that teachers can do the following (adapted from Lieberman et al., 2017, p. 126):

- Identify a priority of professional practice that they are passionate about improving;
- Consider how they are going to learn to improve their own practice, collaborate with others, and share their professional learning;
- Be intentional about how they will lead and engage other teachers in collaborative professional learning and the sharing of practice;
- Contribute to collaborative professional learning activities and wider networks; and
- Utilise practical resources to support the sharing, spread, and implementation of new practices.

My PhD participants confirmed that when it comes to professional learning, there is no broad brush solution. Often, one size fits one.

As discussed in Chapter 6, some teachers are taking back their own learning through blogging, Twitter, and TeachMeets. The UK has borne grassroots movements such as ResearchED, WomenEd, and the New Voices conference. I had the privilege of co-editing the book *Flip the System Australia: What matters in education* (Netolicky et al., 2019), which had as one of its aims the elevating and amplifying of voices from the teaching profession. It builds on the work of Jelmer Evers and René Kneyber (2016), and Lucy Rycroft-Smith and Jean-Louis Dutaut (2018), whose books also combine the contributions of teachers, researchers, and education experts, and thereby promote a subversion of current hierarchies and a democratised view of educational reform. If we take Goodson's (1991) point that teacher classroom practice—the arena that professional learning is so often aiming to improve—is an arena susceptible to teacher anxiety, insecurity, and vulnerability, then it is important to listen to teachers, value their experiences, and capture their voices about life and work.

We should heed Bob Burstow's (2018) call to believe in the capacity of teachers to have the will and skill to improve their practice, and to value and recognise teaching staff as "active and involved professionals rather than robotic technicians" (p. 63). We are not objects that need professional learning done to us, or incomplete entities requiring development by external forces acting upon us. We are capable professionals who are willing and able to take responsibility for our learning. Teachers and school leaders benefit from voice and choice in professional learning. Schools and systems can work from their own contexts to design and slowly iterate models of professional learning that facilitate teacher agency.

Focus on context, culture, and relationships

Opportunities for teachers to learn should occur in environments of high trust and high challenge. For professional learning to be successful, a school needs a blame-free culture that encourages talking about learning and extends the understandings and capabilities of the group as a whole and its individual members. When school professionals trust each other, and feel trusted, they feel safe to be vulnerable, experimental, and engaged in reform initiatives (Bryk & Schneider, 2002). Learning—of children and adults—is fostered within an environment in which teachers are nurtured and aligned with a shared purpose.

Teacher evaluation is unhelpful to teacher learning and should be separated from professional learning. Professional learning needs to be non-judgemental and focused on trust and growth, not tied into evaluation. It requires high support to allow vulnerability and openness, and high challenge in order to support those working in our schools to constantly improve. If teachers and school leaders feel challenged to be their best, and 'held' in a supportive environment in which they are seen as nuanced individuals, schools can develop high functioning cultures of continuous improvement.

Professional learning needs to take into account, and indeed focus on, context, culture, and relationships. The professional learning intervention I studied grew out of its specific school context. From the outset, it had built-in evaluation and consultation points in order to constantly check its appropriateness and effectiveness to its intended purpose and to the school community. This allowed the intervention to be continually refined and ensured that refinements were responses to qualitative and quantitative data, not knee-jerk reactions or decisions made by a few leaders out of touch with what was happening on the ground. Participants were most engaged when they perceived *organisational* identity and purpose to resonate with their *personal* identity and purpose.

The notion of *holonomy* (explained in Chapter 8) is reflected in the coaching intervention's combination of self-direction and organisational direction. Its inception as a strategic intervention, and development through teacher teams, reflects the holonomous balance between that which is individual, self-asserting, self-motivating, and self-modifying, but also influenced by and influencing the collective contextual norms, attitudes, values, and behaviours of their larger wholes. This is consistent with Andy Hargreaves and Michael Fullan's (2012) assertion that professional capital is about individual and collective knowing and doing over time.

My PhD (Netolicky, 2016) does not propose that the coaching intervention model, which emerged out of its specific context, be applied to other schools. Rather, other schools can work from their own contexts to research, pilot, design, and implement a teacher growth model starting from their own mission, vision, values, students, staff, and current structures, going slowly and allowing change to iterate from the bottom up, as well as the top down.

Educational success does not come from copying other schools or systems, but by inquiring into their underpinning principles and practices. Not only does one size not fit all teachers or all leaders, neither does one size fit all schools; any change initiative needs to be borne out of the context from which it emerges. We might know those things that are likely to be more effective, but in the end, looking *within*, instead of *outside* our schools, is where we are likely to find what works for us, our school, our teachers, and our students.

Enable collaboration that is rigorous, purposeful, and sometimes uncomfortable

As Chapter 4 explains, rigorous, intentional, and well-designed professional collaboration can benefit students and teachers, but putting educators in a room together is not enough. Meaningful and sustained development—of individual and collective—can be the outcome of professional collaboration with the clear, shared purpose of improving outcomes for students; and relationships, norms, protocols, processes, and data analysis that allow graceful disagreement, productive conflict, collective responsibility, and peer accountability. We do not need to get along, but we do need to work together.

Worth investing in are professional learning communities, observation and reflection processes, mentoring, and coaching. Also important is the collaborations that occur in the daily work of teachers, such as moderation marking meetings, less formal peer observation, collaboration over curriculum planning, and discussion of research literature. Teachers and school leaders can also feel connected through Edcamps, TeachMeets, unconferences, and professional networks on social media. Working productively with others can allow us to gain insights we would be unable to reap alone.

Teachers, school leaders, scholars, and policymakers can do amazing things when we do them together. In my hometown of Perth, one wonderful local example of the power of collective effort occurred in 2014 at my local train station. A man fell as he was boarding his morning train, and got one leg caught in the gap between the train and the platform edge. Transport staff and morning commuters worked together to alert the driver and get everyone off the train. They then proceeded—working together as a collective—to rock the train carriage in unison, managing to tilt it away from the platform and free the man's leg. He escaped uninjured thanks to what was reported in the news as 'people power.' Then in 2018, when a woman slipped while disembarking at a Boston train station in the USA and got her leg caught between the train and the platform, one man—having seen the viral video of the Perth incident online—encouraged the crowd to begin rocking the train. That woman, too, was freed and uninjured. The actions of the Perth passengers had an impact four years on!

As Bob Garmston and Bruce Wellman (2013) write, "tiny events create major disturbances" (p. 9), with the butterfly effects of our individual actions often unseen or unacknowledged. In education, too, stakeholders can band together for a single purpose: the good of our students. Professional collaboration, done well, can have far reaching effects.

Trust teachers and focus on positive drivers

Marianne Larsen (2010) points to the dual, often unquestioned, discourses surrounding the teaching profession: blame and derision of the teacher as incompetent failure on one hand, and the hero trope of the teacher as saviour of students on the other. She argues that both constructs of the concept of 'teacher' are unhelpful to the profession. Education policy that focuses on the teacher means diverting attention away from wider socio-political and economic problems and honing in on teacher performance and accountability. Ironically, an intensified focus on the teacher has meant that teachers are often not supported by growth-focused professional learning, but are policed, dictated to, and deprofessionalised. This has led to work intensification, exhaustion, and exacerbated levels of stress, anxiety, vulnerability, uncertainty, and frustration within the profession.

There are a number of cautions around attempts to measure the impact of professional learning. The quality of teaching and of teachers is not measurable by tests (Kemmis, 2010), and the impact of professional learning is unlikely to be immediately evident as learning can take time to assimilate and make a difference (Evans, 2019). Additionally, measures of teacher effectiveness are unreliable. When teacher performance measures are linked to job or financial decisions, teachers are unlikely to innovate, tending instead to performance-teach to the evaluation (Wiliam, 2014). Merit pay according to performance against standardised tests or teacher standards, is seen by a number of scholars as an unhelpful intervention that commodifies, oversimplifies, and even demeans, educational practice (Hargreaves & Fullan, 2012; Kemmis, 2010).

Yet many education and professional learning focused reforms foreground competitive or punitive approaches that involve narrow measures of success. Negative drivers of change—such as merit-based, standardised measures—develop toxic cultures of fear and competition, rather than productive cultures of collaboration and learning (Fullan, 2011; Fullan & Quinn, 2016; Kemmis, 2010). A performativity agenda coupled with a test-focused teacher-monitoring system encourages uncritical teacher compliance, reduces teachers' connections with individual students, challenges teachers' identities, and diminishes teachers' senses of motivation, efficacy, job satisfaction, and agency (Day, 2002).

Yong Zhao (2016) acknowledges the strong desire for measuring students, teachers, and schools, but argues for treating numbers with suspicion and expanding what is measured in education. Schools and systems need to work to generate meaningful data on what matters and what they really want to know, rather than what is seductively simple to measure or what is used for often unreliable and invalid comparisons.

Approaches to professional learning would benefit from being driven by those things that: foster motivation, engage people in collaborative, continuous, focused improvement; and have wide-reaching impact (Fullan, 2011; Fullan & Quinn, 2016). Some see a fitting approach to be focusing on building the culture of schools as collaborative professional learning communities that engage in the complexities of practice, in the development of educators' beliefs and practices, and in collective learning culture. Positive change requires national and school cultures that trust teachers, see them as experts, and support them in professional learning that builds efficacy, individual capacity, and collaborative expertise.

There is an important place for evaluation, performance management, and directive consultation, but if the purpose of professional learning is growth and improvement in practice, then the use of systems of merit or punishment that score and rate teachers, are not appropriate. Growth, collaboration, and empowerment are ways into developing educators' learning and the learning cultures of schools.

Education is not a calamitous problem to be solved, a bunch of broken individuals to be fixed, or a commercial opportunity ready to be flooded by corporate solutions. Teachers, school leaders, and schools deserve trust, respect, support, and involvement in policymaking. They deserve a voice in the ways in which education is discussed, conceptualised, and developed. Teacher agency—that is, teachers' active contribution to shaping their work and its conditions—is key to effective professional learning.

Broaden the definition of professional learning

Stephen Brookfield wrote in 1986 that "the teaching-learning transactions undertaken by adults are complex and multifaceted, and they steadfastly refuse simple categorisation. They occur in every setting imaginable, … and involve a range of formats and methods" (pp. 1–2). Learning experiences can be 'molten': chaotic, complex, and ambiguous, resulting from multiple overlapping experiences operating together (Allen & Kayes, 2012). My PhD study (Netolicky, 2016), as elucidated in Chapter 3, suggests that transformational professional learning can occur in unexpected ways and places. A range of epiphanic life experiences can shape professional identities and practices. As my PhD participants explained, it is often not those experiences labelled *professional learning* or *professional development* which are transformational for educators, but experiences of life, relationships, and emotions. Teachers and leaders in my study explained how their beliefs and practices had shifted through experiences such as listening to an inspiring speaker, being managed by an ineffective leader, doing volunteer work, being a parent, completing a Masters, or travelling to third world countries and seeing the realities of life for others around the world.

Teachers and school leaders build their learning out of experiences, but also out of identities. Educators' professional identities might be shaped by learning which focuses, not only on ways to improve practice, but on the kind of teacher it is possible to be (Mockler, 2011). It is learning that taps into who educators perceive that they are that seems to have the most impact on belief, thought, behaviour, and therefore practice.

The revelation that professional learning encompasses a wide range of lifelong experiences impacts how schools and systems might consider professional learning. It points to a need to broaden the definition of professional learning, to allow teachers and schools to think more expansively and flexibly about what it is that transforms educators professionally, and who drives and chooses this learning. Bob Burstow (2018) challenges designers and providers of educator professional learning to consider where professional learning opportunities are situated on axes of individual to organisation, bottom up to top down, and theory to practice.

I argue that the definition of professional learning be expanded from traditional school and educational learning experiences, and that the scope of studying professional learning be broadened. Education systems, policymakers, teaching associations, professional learning providers, schools, and school leaders can look to teachers and leaders themselves for their perceptions of when learning had been transformational. They might consider alternate possibilities for educators' learning opportunities, especially those that involve educators' notions of self. Opportunities can be provided for educators to place themselves and their lived experiences squarely in the centre of their own self-directed learning. Verbal and written reflection and conversation, whether through collaborative groups, coaching conversations, blogs, microblogging, interviews, or online communities, can be built into professional learning in order to focus individuals on how their learning knits together with the fabric of their professional identity and with their community. Schools and systems would likely benefit from considering, acknowledging, and allowing exploration of identity in professional learning endeavours.

Invest time, money, and resources

One thing teachers and school leaders are short on is time. We often do not have the mental space to embed professional learning in our practice, or indeed to think deeply about problems of practice. Racing from class to class, to meeting, to duty, to after school club, to parents' evening, is not conducive to a profession who can reflect on our beliefs, our practice, and our learning. This was evident when the school leaders in my PhD study thanked me for the time and space to sit down during the research interviews, and talk about their leadership beliefs, experiences, and decision making.

Teachers and school leaders need time to consider our beliefs, practices, and professional identities, and to develop theoretical understandings and congruent practices. We need time to collaborate meaningfully, or to step away from the busyness of daily responsibilities in order to process our learning. Protecting time for teacher and school leader wellbeing and mental space is key to growth, allowing reflection away from the relentlessness of the school day.

There is an African proverb that suggests: 'If you want to go fast, go alone. If you want to go far, go together.' Applying the kernel of this proverb to education, is to consider slow, collaborative, intentional, and well-resourced professional learning over often knee-jerk, ineffective attempts at fast, often under-resourced change. In the education world of fast policy, fast reform, fast solutions and fast measurement, what is needed it to go deliberately and incrementally. In the example of education policy, Steven Lewis and Anna Hogan (2016) argue against reactive, short term policy and advocate for slow policy that is considered, thoughtful, and acknowledges local cultures, histories, and conditions. Professional learning initiatives, too, need a 'go slow' approach. This includes adequate training, sufficient time, appropriate resources, and a process to review the effectiveness of the initiative.

Often, systems and schools struggle to prioritise or accommodate the resourcing necessary for effective professional learning to occur. The Australian Gonski 2.0 report (Gonski et al., 2018) points out that teachers are weighed down by administrivia and tasks additional to their teaching load. The report notes that "submissions to the Review argued that teachers want to focus on teaching" (p. 60) and suggests that schools will need to rethink "time use and work practices … where the average teacher is often burdened with administrative tasks and finds little time to develop new teaching skills," for instance by "considering different and innovative ways to free up teacher time, for example using more paid paraprofessionals and other non-teaching personnel, including trained volunteers, to assist with non-teaching tasks such as lunchtime or assembly supervision or administrative tasks" (p. 57). Most teachers, however, will attest to more and more expectations—such as to collaborate more rigorously and regularly with other teachers, to read current research, to interrogate and act upon increasing swathes of data—being added onto the work of teachers, with little or nothing being removed. Many teachers attend professional development activities in their holidays or on their weekends, and sometimes at their own cost.

So, in the Australian context, teachers are crying out for more time to focus on their core business of teaching, including by collaborating with other teachers. Meanwhile, North American teachers spend much more time—80% of their time, in fact—teaching students, with significantly less time to plan and learn together, and to develop high quality curriculum and instruction (Darling-Hammond et al., 2009). In Canada, common challenges to professional learning include finding time within the work day, access and funding inequities, and contentions in the balance between system-directed and self-selected professional learning for teachers (Campbell et al., 2017). Andy Hargreaves and Michael O'Connor (2018) point out that most texts on professional learning end with advocacy for better leadership, more time, and more resources. Let me say it here once more, with feeling: education reforms and professional learning need sufficient time and prudently planned resourcing.

Time and resourcing means more than identifying a professional learning program and throwing money at it. Professional collaboration, coaching or mentoring relationships, and ongoing learning opportunities such as postgraduate study, need time. Teachers need structural support to make time for effective learning that isn't about compliance or counting PD hours, but about immersion in activities that can transform their beliefs and practices. If systems and schools are to prioritise professional learning that makes a difference, they must consider not only money and resourcing, but where in teachers' workloads time can be clawed back for this important work.

Final thoughts

As this book has shown, professional learning is a broad field, but not a straightforward one. Its size and complexity means that many definitions (such as of terms like *mentoring, coaching*, and *professional learning communities*) have become loose, contradictory, or contested. The profession is not always speaking the same language when we use particular words. Some words become buzz words that lose all meaning but become ubiquitous in conversations around education: *data, evidence-based, mindset*. These fly from the mouths of educators, consultants, and media commentators, but without a shared understanding.

We need to work towards a shared and deep understanding of terms, not merely pay lip-service to the latest craze or popular approach. We need to ask good questions of system leaders, school leaders, and those touting professional learning products and services. This book is an attempt to tease out and explain in some detail approaches to professional learning that can make a difference in schools.

There is an endless array of professional learning topics in education, from pedagogy and student wellbeing, to coaching and subject specific courses. No one teacher can ever know it all, and no one school can ever focus on it all, so there is always something to sell, and to buy. There are always deficiencies to be found by opportunists with questionable agendas (Waite, 2016) amid the range of complex intersecting phenomena of schooling and education. It can always be argued that nations, districts, schools, and teachers can do better, more, differently. Innovation, disruption, and entrepreneurship all feed the narrative that there is a new, shiny, better way to 'do' education or to be an educator.

One of the key messages of this book is to believe in the capacity of teachers and school leaders, and to trust them to do their jobs. There is excellent work going on in our schools, in Australia and around the world. We can build on this by investing in professional learning that makes a difference to students and staff in schools. We shouldn't shy away from complexity or try to dumb down professional learning for teachers. Yes, teachers and school leaders are time poor, but we are also intelligent professionals with the capacity to learn, grow, and best serve the students in our care.

Understanding what makes effective and transformational professional learning is important if we are to best serve our schools, school leaders, teachers, and students. The *Australian Charter for the professional learning of teachers and school leaders* (AITSL, 2012) reflects the sentiments of education systems around the world when it states that "high quality professional learning is central to improving the quality of teaching, and through this to improving the outcomes we achieve for all young Australians" (p. 6). As the extensive, but by no means exhaustive, reference lists of this book attest, there are document after document, text after text, policy after policy, that attempt to capture what 'high quality professional learning' is, what effects it has, how to implement it, and how to scale it up to system level.

We need to be willing to engage in social, collaborative, and cultural professional capital. This relational and cultural work is more difficult and complex than more simplistic technical steps, but is essential if we are to engage transformational rather than merely transactional learning. Those leading professional learning in our schools can consider internal experts as well as looking to external expertise outside our school walls. We can look to local and global networks to build common understandings. Let's trust our own people. Champion and develop what they know and can do. Think deeply about the wide variety of possible opportunities to support the growth and development of those staff in our care, with a view to enhance the experience and improve the learning of students. And let's not forget that teachers are human beings with bodies, minds, complex personal lives, professional identities, frailties, and deep-seated beliefs about themselves and about teaching and learning. As teachers and school leaders, we are not cookie cutter clones but diverse human beings with a range of motivations, family responsibilities, aspirations, and professional as well as personal needs. If we are adding to teachers' workloads we need to think about what we can take away.

As in other education fields, the answer to the question "What works?" is often "It depends." However, accepting the complexities and nuances of professional learning does not preclude us from knowing what is likely to be effective, and in what kinds of professional learning schools would benefit from investing. Professional learning that makes a difference concentrates on growth and support of teachers in order to positively impact students. It should not be based on performance and punishment.

Transformational professional learning can occur in a wide range of life arenas. The best professional learning can be more than collaborative, targeted, and ongoing, as suggested by much research literature. It can look different for different individuals, teams, and schools, depending on career stage, context, school sector, and circumstance.

Transformational professional learning should be a priority, for the learning of our students, but also for the wellbeing, energy, motivation, and professionalism of our teachers and school leaders. As Sally Zepeda (2013) claims, "professional development cannot be left to chance" (p. 64). Transformational learning moments are "the birthplace's of our life's work" (Shuler et al., 2017, p. vii) and so I argue here for a focus on professional learning for educators that is transformational rather than transactional; about growth not compliance; and simultaneously taking into account the individual, the group, the organisation, and the system.

The role of those leading professional learning—at school, district, and national levels—is to support professional learning that really makes a difference to teachers and school leaders, and therefore to students and schools. Treating each staff member as an individual adult learner is more difficult than sending everyone to a course and hoping it sticks, or posting the latest league table of apparently effective teaching strategies to the staff room wall. It is as complex and nuanced as the people in our schools. But there are clear places we should look if we want to shape the beliefs of teachers and leaders, and thereby shift practice. We can focus on supported reflection, goal setting, and planning for individual staff; collaboration that is rigorous, purposeful, and sometimes uncomfortable; and on ensuring professional learning is a serious consideration in terms of time and resources.

Professional learning is not collecting hours or notches on a resume. It is at the heart of the teaching profession and the foundation stone of student learning and achievement.

References

Allen, N., & Kayes, D. C. (2012). Leader development in dynamic and hazardous environments: Company commander learning through combat. In A. Mc Kee & M. Eraut (Eds.). *Learning trajectories, innovation and identity for professional development* (pp. 93–111). Dordrecht: Springer.

Australian Institute for Teaching and School Leadership (AITSL). (2012). *Australian Charter for the professional learning of teachers and school leaders.* Carlton South: Education Council.

Ball, S. J. (2016). Subjectivity as a site of struggle: Refusing neoliberalism? *British Journal of Sociology of Education, 37*(8), 1129–1146.

Brookfield, S. D. (1986). *Understanding and facilitating adult learning: A comprehensive analysis of principles and effective practices.* Buckingham: Open University Press.

Bryk, A., & Schneider, B. (2002). *Trust in schools: A core resource for improvement.* New York: Russell Sage Foundation.

Burstow, B. (2018). *Effective teacher development: Theory and practice in professional learning.* London: Bloomsbury.

Campbell, C., Osmond-Johnson, P., Faubert, B., Zeichner, K., & Hobbs-Johnson, A. (2017). *The state of educators' professional learning in Canada: Final research report.* Oxford: Learning Forward.

Darling-Hammond, L., Wei, R. C., Andree, A., Richardson, N., & Orphanos, S. (2009). *Professional learning in the learning profession.* Washington: National Staff Development Council.

Day, C. (2002). School reform and transitions in teacher professionalism and identity. *International Journal of Educational Research, 37*(8), 677–692.

Evans, L. (2019). Implicit and informal professional development: What it 'looks like', how it occurs, and why we need to research it. *Professional Development in Education, 45*(1), 3–16.

Evers, J., & Kneyber, R. (Eds.). (2016). *Flip the system: Changing education from the ground up.* Abingdon: Routledge.

Fullan, M. (2011). Choosing the wrong drivers for whole school reform. *Seminar Series, 204.*

Fullan, M., & Quinn, J. (2016). *Coherence: The right drivers in action for schools, districts, and systems.* Thousand Oaks: Corwin.

Garmston, R. J., & Wellman, B. (2013). *Adaptive schools: A sourcebook for developing collaborative groups* (2nd ed.). Lanham: Rowman & Littlefield.

Gonski, D., Arcus, T., Boston, K., Gould, V., Johnson, W., O'Brien, L., … Roberts, M. (2018). *Through growth to achievement: The report of the review to achieve educational excellence in Australian schools.* Canberra: Commonwealth of Australia.

Goodson, I. F. (1991). Teachers' lives and educational research. In I. F. Goodson & R. Walker (Eds.). *Biography, identity and schooling: Episodes in educational research* (pp. 137–149). London: Falmer.

Hargreaves, A., & Fullan, M. (2012). *Professional capital: Transforming teaching in every school.* Moorabbin: Hawker Brownlow Education.

Hargreaves, A., & O'Connor, M. T. (2018). *Collaborative professionalism: When teaching together means learning for all.* Thousand Oaks: Corwin.

Keddie, A. (2017). School autonomy reform and public education in Australia: Implications for social justice. *The Australian Educational Researcher, 44*(4-5), 373–390.

Kemmis, S. (2010). What is professional practice? In C. Kanes (Ed.). *Elaborating professionalism: Studies in practice and theory* (pp. 130–166). London: Springer.

Larsen, M. A. (2010). Troubling the discourse of teacher centrality: A comparative perspective. *Journal of Education Policy, 25*(2), 207–231.

Lewis, S., & Hogan, A. (2016). Reform first and ask questions later? The implications of (fast) schooling policy and 'silver bullet' solutions. *Critical Studies in Education, 60*(1), 1–18.

Lieberman, A., Campbell, C., & Yashkina, A. (2017). *Teacher leadership and learning: Of, by, and for teachers.* Abingdon: Routledge.

Mockler, N. (2011). Becoming and 'being' a teacher: Understanding teacher professional identity. In N. Mockler & J. Sachs (Eds.). *Rethinking educational practice through reflexive inquiry* (pp. 123–138). Dordrecht: Springer.

Netolicky, D. M. (2016). *Down the rabbit hole: Professional identities, professional learning, and change in one Australian school* (Doctoral dissertation, Murdoch University).

Netolicky, D. M., Andrews, J., & Paterson, C. (Eds.). (2019). *Flip the system Australia: What matters in education.* Abingdon: Routledge.

Rycroft-Smith, L., & Dutaut, J. L. (Eds.). (2018). *Flip the system UK: A teachers' manifesto.* Abingdon: Routledge.

Senge, P. M. (2012). *Schools that learn: A fifth discipline fieldbook for educators, parents and everyone who cares about education* (2nd ed.). London: Nicholas Brearley.

Shuler, M. K., Keller-Dupree, E., & Cook, K. (Eds.). (2017). *Transformational learning experiences: A conversation with counsellors and their personal and professional development journeys*. Lanham: Hamilton Books.

Timperley, H. (2008). *Teacher professional learning and development: Educational practices series 18*. Brussels: International Academy of Education, International Bureau of Education & UNESCO.

van Nieuwerburgh, C. (2016). Towards a coaching culture. In C. van Nieuwerburgh (Ed.). *Coaching in professional contexts* (pp. 227–234). London: Sage.

Waite, D. (2016). Of charlatans, sorcerers, alchemists, demagogues, profit-mongers, tyrants and kings: Educational reform and the death by a thousand cuts. *The Urban Review, 48*(1), 123–148.

Wiliam, D. (2014). The formative evaluation of teaching performance. (Occasional Paper 137). East Melbourne, Australia: Centre for Strategic Education.

Wiliam, D. (2018). *Creating the schools our children need: Why what we're doing now won't help much (and what we can do instead)*. Palm Beach: Learning Sciences.

Zepeda, S. J. (2013). *Professional development: What works* (2nd ed.). New York: Routledge.

Zhao, Y. (2016). Numbers can lie: The meaning and limitations of test scores. In Y. Zhao (Ed.). *Counting what counts: Reframing education outcomes* (pp. 13–29). Bloomington: Solution Tree.

Appendices

Appendix A: Details of the PhD study cited in this book

Throughout this book I reference my PhD study, which I completed between 2012 and 2016. In this Appendix I provide further details of the study so that readers can understand the study from which data and conclusions in this book were drawn.

The study's context

The study was set against the backdrop of the global push for better teaching and better student achievement. Education systems and schools had their eyes firmly on standardised test scores. The terms 'teacher quality,' 'quality teaching' and 'teaching effectiveness' were being used to denote the quality of teachers' teaching, in terms of its effectiveness in adding value to student learning, as measured by standardised, often high stakes, tests. There were resulting impacts on education policy and practice, with new teacher evaluation systems being rolled out across the USA, talk of performance based pay for teachers, and initiatives in professional development around the world promising to make teachers and their teaching better. Around the world, the media were reporting on global education rankings based on tests such as PISA. Who was at the top? Who was lagging behind or falling behind?

The research questions

My PhD study generated context-specific interview data in order to answer the questions:

a) What is the role of professional learning on identities or growth?; and
b) What professional learning is transformational?

It examined the experiences of a group of educators against the catalytic context of one well-resourced, independent, Australian school's professional growth model. The beginning of coaching intervention in 2013 provided a unique time and place against which to set a study of professional learning. Looking more broadly than the studied intervention, at participants' lifelong learning experiences, this study took an insider look at the underexplored perceptions of teachers and combined this with the views of school leaders, including middle leaders who are often absent from research literature. Interviews of me as researcher (also an educator at the school), two teachers, and 11 school leaders, illuminated what learning might be considered professionally transformational in shaping educators' beliefs and practices.

The study, positioned within a social constructionist theoretical frame and focused on the phenomenon of transformational professional learning, sought a method that would provide in-depth insights into teachers' and school leaders' perceptions of their learning. Narrative method was selected to align with the purpose and ontology of the study and to provide in-depth insights into lived experiences. It privileges humanness and the plurality of truths, harnessing remembrance and retelling as a way into understanding phenomena, and into uncovering significance in our remembered moments. In this case, the study asked participants to share their experiences of professional learning across their lives and within the context of a school-based intervention.

Site: my school

The research site for the present study was my then-school. It is an Australian, non-selective, independent, well-resourced Pre-Kindergarten to Year 12 school, with about 1500 students from metropolitan, rural, and international back-grounds. The commencement of the school's coaching intervention, explained below, provided a timely opportunity for teachers and academic leaders to reflect on their experiences of professional learning as part of a study that occurred alongside, but separate to, the studied intervention.

The intervention context: the coaching intervention

The coaching intervention, a teacher-directed growth-through-observation-and-coaching intervention, situated within the context of the school, provided a backdrop for this study's participants and their stories of professional learning. The coaching intervention was a new intervention in 2013 that used a combination of cognitive coaching and the Danielson Framework for Teaching as a model of professional conversation and formalised reflection on teaching practice. The intervention was not a stand-alone reform but was introduced alongside already-existing work such as use of the Danielson Framework for Teaching in teacher-self-reflection documents, professional learning community teams, and the work of external pedagogical consultants with classroom teachers.

The model of learning being explored by the teachers involved in the coaching intervention included use of the Danielson Framework for Teaching within a coaching-and-observation cycle using cognitive coaching. The annual cycle involved the following steps:

1. **Self-reflect**: Teacher coachee completes self-reflection against Danielson Framework for Teaching.
2. **Touch base**: Preconference with coach, identifying possible foci, deciding on type of lesson data to be collected.

3. **Generate lesson data**: 2 x 20-minute lesson observations with non-judgemental data generation via written scripting, mapping, video recording, or audio recording.
4. **Reflect and plan**: Post conference cognitive coaching conversation using the Danielson Framework for Teaching for teacher self-reflection.
5. **Repeat 2, 3, and 4**.

A cognitive coaching approach was chosen by the school for its emphasis on building internal capacity and self-actualisation; coaches were seen as experts in coaching to develop coachees' thinking, not givers of advice or providers of solutions. Coaching intervention teacher-members were trained in cognitive coaching by an agency trainer for Thinking Collaborative, the body which provides the official cognitive coaching course. The first coaching intervention members, a team of 13 teacher volunteers from across year levels and faculties, including me as researcher and intervention facilitator, coached each other as they developed the school's model of professional learning. In 2014 the coaching intervention team of 12 teacher volunteers, including me, coached each other and also 12 additional teachers (who volunteered to be coached and to provide feedback to the school via focus groups and an anonymous survey). In 2015 and 2016 the team of coaches each coached approximately eight teachers per year, as well as coaching and meta-coaching each other.

This study took place during 2013 and 2014, the first two years of the coaching intervention. I was involved in the school's intervention as the person who wrote the school's proposal paper in 2012 and the facilitator of that intervention from 2013–2016. While the participants were selected from my school and the coaching intervention in which she was immersed, this study was not intended as an evaluation of the intervention. The teams responsible for the intervention were involved at a school level in collecting data to evaluate its impacts. Any data collected in my role as facilitator of the intervention was not part of my PhD study. Rather, the intervention acted as a background context to the generation of teacher and leader stories of professional learning.

Participants: researcher, teachers, and school leaders

Participants were drawn from a pool of those involved in the coaching intervention. They were: me as researcher (also a teacher at the school, the facilitator of the intervention, and a participating coach and coachee), two teachers from the intervention, six middle leaders, and five executive leaders. All 12 team members in the first pilot year of the coaching intervention were invited to participate in this study. Four of those teachers volunteered, although two later withdrew. All 19 academic leaders at the school were invited to participate; five executive leaders and six middle leaders agreed.

Data generation

Data were generated in individual, semi-structured narrative-eliciting interviews that posed open, story-inviting questions. The sparing questions—mainly "Tell me about your experience of professional learning" and "Tell me about your experience of the coaching intervention"—were designed to encourage participants to tell their own stories around their experiences of professional learning and the coaching intervention, including its cognitive coaching and Danielson Framework for Teaching elements. Interviews followed a cognitive coaching pattern of 'pause, paraphrase, pause, pose question,' allowing data to reflect the idiosyncrasies of participant stories. The focus on paraphrasing participant responses as part of the narrative listening was an in-interview veracity checking measure; participants were able to immediately approve or amend the way in which their stories were being understood.

The teachers and myself as researcher were interviewed twice by an independent interviewer in the first pilot year of the intervention (2013), while the leaders were interviewed once by me in the second pilot year (2014).

Data analysis

Transcriptions of interviews provided the primary data of the study and were coded for emerging themes, as well as for outlying perspectives. The study took a hermeneutic approach to data interpretation that involved iteratively, immersively studying data for what was meaningful for participants and what themes emerged, using a combination of inductive and deductive interpretive procedures. I conducted an ongoing circle of analysis, repeatedly revisiting data, looking for converging patterns and individual divergences.

Ethical measures

Ethics underpins the research process and requires constant decision making, and a combination of problem solving and creativity. As a research I contended with the ethical tensions of protecting participants' anonymity while communicating authentic data, especially when researching a small community of potential participants, as in the case of this study. In this case, my insider role, especially that of member and facilitator of the coaching intervention, meant that ethical risks to the (especially teacher) participants needed to be minimised. Teacher participants, due to their more vulnerable position as part of the coaching intervention team, were more stringently protected than the school leaders, who were in a less vulnerable position.

In order to protect teacher participants, I was deliberately kept from knowing which of the 11 teachers volunteered, which did not volunteer, or subsequently which participants withdrew. The process involved me emailing the coaching intervention team in May of 2013 to inform them of, and invite them to participate in, the study. Teachers were instructed to email their intention to volunteer, not to me as researcher, but to a third party, who took on the role of communicating with the teacher participants and keeping their identities concealed from me. In order to address the issue of conflicts of interest, dependency, risks to those who chose not to participate, and the complexity of my embeddedness in the research context, an independent interviewer interviewed teacher participants, after being briefed by me about protocols and questions. This independent interviewer had no connection with the research site or the participants and was bound by a confidentiality agreement. As researcher, I was interviewed first, before the teachers, in order to give the independent interviewer a better understanding of the research being undertaken. This approach to interviewing helped to enhance authenticity by minimising relationship complexities between interviewer and interviewee, helping to build rapport, trust, and openness, giving participants more scope to express the way they saw things.

After teacher interviews were conducted, audio recorded interview data were then transcribed and de-identified. That is, a third party removed any identifying details from transcripts, then sent them to participants for authentication. This step in veracity checking allowed teachers to approve or amend the transcripts before the de-identified, authenticated transcriptions were provided to me. As I only received de-identified transcripts of interviews, vulnerability, relationships, and professional risks to both those involved in the research, and those not involved in the research, were lessened. That only four of 11 teachers volunteered to participate, and that two withdrew, reflects the possibility that participants involved in narrative research may feel vulnerable, exposed, or at risk of having themselves and their data identified.

School leaders were interviewed once by me. As the school leaders were not in a dependent relationship with me, it was not deemed as necessary for interviews to be undertaken by an independent interviewer. There were, however, still ethical complexities; in some cases, I was line managed by these leaders, and in others I was independent of them. Furthermore, position alone does not equate to a lack of vulnerability. In order to address issues of dependency and minimise work relationship issues, school leaders were informed (in letters and at the beginning of the interview) that they did not have to answer any question with which they feel uncomfortable, could withdraw from the interview or study at any time, and would be given the opportunity to authenticate interview transcripts. I made clear my separate role of researcher, as distinct from my role in the school, and that all data generated would remain anonymous and confidential.

Limitations

This study may be seen as limited by its specific context, its small unrepresentative sample of participants, and its limited duration. Unlike other research which has been undertaken in disadvantaged or government schools, this study examined participants within the context of a well-funded independent school. The school had the resources to spend time and money on an initiative like the coaching intervention. It was willing and able to allocate a staff member, in this case me, to lead that intervention. This meant that in my school role I was responsible for leading the intervention, presenting to the school board, selecting a team, and coordinating their work. It also meant that teachers were given a time or monetary incentive to participate in the intervention. This is a very specific set of circumstances, which cannot be generalised to all schools, teachers, and school leaders.

Studying 14 participants narrowed the study's focus to the experiences of those people. Not only that, but the teacher participants were volunteer members of a school-based intervention, suggesting that they were not a representative sample of the teachers at the school as a whole, a point that the participants themselves identified. That these participants were volunteers, means that the study was unable to consider the perspectives of those whose identities do not fit within their school and who feel alienated from the values and practices of their organisation. The data also reveal the school as an organisation was perceived by participants as aligned with their own identities; it would be unlikely that this would extend to all teachers at the school. The small unrepresentative sample, while allowing my study to reach a deep understanding of phenomena from very specific perspectives, makes transferability problematic.

Narrative inquiry as used in my PhD study, has, like any method, its strengths and limitations. While the study aimed to present participant stories in ways that were faithful to and respectful of those stories, like much qualitative analysis which is dependent on the perceptions and words of people, the participant data of this study are limited to participant experience, full of the complexity of being human, and may not be logically or factually consistent. Data analysis could only focus on what was said; not those details participants chose to omit or those stories not told. The data generated are also influenced by interview questions, the interviewer, and transcription decisions, as well as the choices made in reporting on the research. Some argue, however, that personal narratives are of interest precisely because narrators interpret the past in stories, rather than reproducing it. Narrative data can help to illuminate an understanding of lived experience and people's perceptions of it, revealing internal truths of lived experience.

Generating data over a two-year period means that the present study provides a microanalytic view of the beginning of a school-based intervention, rather than providing insights into how it evolved over an extended period of time. As I have continued to be a teacher, coach, coaching intervention leader, and overseer of professional learning after data generation for this study was finished, I can see the benefit of taking a more longitudinal view than a time-constrained PhD study allows. In my school role, since finishing this study's data generation, I have watched the coaching intervention develop into a fully implemented, whole school model of observation-and-coaching-conversation based growth. Continuing to be an insider at the school has shown me the potential for applying an approach like that used in this study for longer periods, to track individual and organisational change over time, and canvas a wider variety of perspectives.

The final limitation of the research may be considered to be me, the researcher, embedded as I was in the context of the research as a teacher and middle leader at the school and the facilitator of the coaching intervention. My insider perspective may have influenced the reactivity of the participants, as well as influencing the interpretation and reporting of data. Yet in examining 14 individuals in one school, from three participant groups, the study was able to provide deep insights into teachers' and leaders' lived experiences of professional learning. While some may view my insider-outsider subjectivity as limiting, it can be seen as an important lens through which to view school reform and educator perspectives: from within the school system rather than outside it.

Appendix B: Implementation timeline for the coaching intervention

The coaching model discussed in Chapter 5 required high level conceptual, strategic and operational thinking. The following table shows the three-year roll out of the model, which continues to operate within a recently reimagined professional learning framework.

The coaching mode remains at the time of writing, but is now part of a more differentiated model of school-based professional learning that involves more staff choice of a greater number of options.

Table A.1 Implementation timeline for the coaching intervention

Year	Coaching intervention
2012	**Proposal year** (July) I wrote a school proposal paper for the coaching initiative, with rationale from research and the school context. It included investigation of quality teaching, how it can be recognised, and what research suggests about what works in improving it; as well as literature on effectives school change. (August) I presented the proposal paper to the school board, including recommendations for a pilot model that involved cycles of lesson observations and coaching conversations, using the Danielson Framework for Teaching and cognitive coaching (choices based in research evidence and school context, vision, and values). (November) I presented to academic staff on the pilot coaching intervention and called for volunteers. 25 teachers volunteered. 11 teachers were selected by the principal for the 2013 coaching intervention team based on: forming a group of individuals small enough to be optimal for effective team work; individual teachers' situations; and the desire to include a diverse range of teachers, including those from early learning to senior secondary; in career stages from novice to veteran; and from a variety of learning areas.
2013	**First pilot year: Coaching intervention** (Across the year) The coaching intervention team was trained by a Danielson Group consultant in the Danielson Framework for Teaching and in taking non-inferential lesson observation data. The team was trained in cognitive coaching by an agency trainer for Thinking Collaborative. Team members observed each other's lessons and coached each other. Team members designed and trialed a survey instrument for tracking teacher self-perceptions against the Danielson Framework for Teaching. (October–November) The team designed its recommended teacher growth model. I presented the model to the principal and school board. The team requested a further pilot year to test and refine the model. (December) Called for volunteers for second pilot year of the intervention. 13 teachers volunteered; all 13 were accepted to be part of the second pilot year team, led by me.

(Continued)

Table A.1 (Cont.)

Year	Coaching intervention

2014 Second pilot year: Coaching intervention

(Across the year) The new coaching intervention team was trained by a Danielson Group consultant in the Danielson Framework for Teaching and in taking non-inferential lesson observation data. The new team trained in cognitive coaching by an agency trainer for Thinking Collaborative. Team members observed each other's lessons and coached each other. The team additionally worked in sub-committees to develop: plans and resources for data generation and analysis of the intervention work; human resources processes and documentation; alignment of the Danielson Framework with the Australian National Professional Standards for Teachers; and a clear model for implementation from 2015.

(July–October) Teachers outside the team were asked to volunteer to be coached by the team. 14 teachers volunteered and participated in a coaching cycle (pre-observation conversation – multiple short lesson observations and data collection – reflecting into planning conversation).

(October) Focus groups and surveys of team members and their volunteer coachees. Human resources processes for implementation in 2015 finalised. Danielson Framework for Teaching alignment crosswalk with AITSL National Professional Standards completed. Teacher pre-survey designed. Data generation plan complete. Report submitted to the school board.

(November) Invitation for teachers to apply for the position of Teacher Coach. Eight coaches selected by me and the Director of Teaching and Learning, via an interview process that included conducting a coaching conversation and answering interview questions. Six coaches were previous members of the coaching intervention pilot teams.

2015 First implementation year: Coaching model for all

(January) With Human Resources, I organised coaching pairs across the school; all academic staff except managers were assigned a coach.

(February–April) All teachers completed an initial online reflection against the Danielson Framework for Teaching, which we had designed. All coaches and all academic leaders were trained by a Danielson Group consultant in the Danielson Framework for Teaching, in taking non-inferential lesson observation data. Coaches and managers were trained in cognitive coaching by an agency trainer for Thinking Collaborative.

(October) Focus groups with coaches and managers. Anonymous survey of coachees.

(November) Refinement of model, processes, and documentation for 2016 including differentiation for academic leaders.

2016 Second implementation year: Coaching model differentiated for teachers and leaders

(January) With Human Resources, I organised coaching pairs across the school; all academic staff were assigned a coach.

(Across the year) I continued to lead the team of coaches, and also coach teachers and leaders to improve their practice. I organised a visit by Bruce Wellman to work with coaches and leaders on coaching, navigating continua of interaction, and using data. I worked with others to refine the coaching model, upgrade appraisal and capacity-building processes, and develop a leadership framework.

Index

time, money and resources, investment of 128–9
timing and process of learning 26–7
Timperley, H. 26, 33, 79, 122; et al. 5, 22, 23, 52
TNTP report, USA 25–6
travel 43–5
trust: in coaching relationship 69, 71, 74; leaders, role of 103–4; in teaching profession 125–7, 130
Tuckman, B. 50
Twitter/tweeting 45, 80–1, 82, 123

USA 8, 17, 23, 24, 25–6, 33, 54, 122; Measures for Effective Teaching (MET) 90; national standards 88

value of approach 129–31; and limitations 25–6

van Nieuwerburgh, C. 122–3; and Passmore, J. 70
Visible Learning (Hattie) 105–6
vision: shared 110–12; and strategic direction 112
voice, choice and space 122–3
volunteering 42–3

Warren Little, J. 47
Whitmore, J. 64
wider life experiences 41–3
Wilkinson, J. and Kemmis, S. 103
Wiliam, D. 67, 90–1, 121
workshops 33, 35–6, 48, 116
writing 81–3

Yoon, K. S. 25; et al. 33, 34

Zepeda, S. 22, 53–4, 131; et al. 65, 66, 79